Short Stories

by

Thomas Ryan

Far and Wide
publishing

www.thomasryanwriter.com

New Zealand National Library
ISBN 978-0-473-25721-7

For Archie and Hugo

Nightmares... *'Fabulous'*

Ruth... *'No doubt about it. Thomas Ryan is the real McCoy. It zings along'*

The Artist.... *'I enjoyed your story, good twist in there too'*

The Dementia Man... *'I just enjoyed your short story. I thought I saw the end coming, but you doubled-back on me'*

Ruth... *'An astonishing tale! I nearly fell out of my chair at the last paragraph! Thanks for sharing'*

Acknowledgements

I need to thank my long time writers' group who critiqued my work and helped guide me through the process of arranging my words into legible order, Trisha Hanifin, Sue Gee, Meemee Phipps, Karen Van Eden, Miles Hughes. Cover design is by selfpubbookcovers.com/RLSather. My gratitude to Stephanie Dagg from Edit-My-Book for proof editing and polish, and Ron Davis who helped craft the final touches.

Mostly I want to thank my long suffering wife Meg for her continuing support and who is owed such a debt of gratitude it would be impossible to repay.

Stories

Ruth

After hitting the kitchen floor and suffering the sickening sensation of her head bouncing off the grey slate, Ruth Deverett found her vision blurry. Squinting eyes couldn't make out the position of the hands on the wall clock above the fridge. No matter. She knew it was six o'clock. There was no mistaking the news signature tune streaming from the television set in the lounge.

And the day?

Easy.

From the cheese and garlic aromas in her nostrils, the dish now splattered across the floor could only have been lasagna. Robert demanded she keep a strict mealtime regimen. Roast on Sunday, steak on Monday, curry on Tuesday and….

Lasagna on Wednesday.

So, Wednesday it was.

A cautious hand lifted from the tiles and drew up the rough weave of her husband-prescribed white linen apron. Tips of fingers gently patted the side of her head. A wince as Ruth encountered a newly formed lump.

Her head never used to jar this badly when it hit vinyl. She had argued with Robert against replacing the vinyl, but as usual a forceful justification of the soundness of his decision had silenced her. How fortunate, Ruth continually reminded herself, to have a husband who was so supremely confident of the correctness of his opinions.

Out the corner of her eye she caught sight of a movement. A defensive hand flew to her side. A boot deflected off her wrist and into her thigh. Needles of pain stabbed through her upper arm. She knew another blow would come and squeezed her eyes tight. She worried her wrist might be broken. How could she iron Robert's shirt in the morning with a broken wrist? Her own fault really, she should not have tried to defend herself. Robert had repeatedly yelled at her not to do so. It only made him angrier.

She should apologise for her foolishness. After all, Robert only ever offered helpful advice.

Without opening her eyes Ruth curled into a fetal position and waited. The toe of Robert's boot tapped against the table leg. She sensed him looking down at her, almost certainly disgusted by her weakness and deliberating his next move. This usually meant he was calming. She held her breath, guarding against sound. A groan would set him off again. She ached, but it wasn't so bad. Not as bad as other times.

She heard the news reader introduce a news bulletin.

That meant the ad break was over. Robert would not miss the news, not on her account.

A bowl smashed against the wall. Ruth flinched. Lettuce and tomato sprinkled across her exposed calf. Shards of crockery skittered across the floor. This was a good sign. Robert only threw dishes at the wall when it was over. A final vent. Footsteps moved away from her. The sound became muffled. He'd reached the thickness of the broadloom carpet in the sitting room.

"Don't move yet," she whispered. "Not yet."

The echoing slam of a fist on desktop.

Eyes fixed on the righteous glare bedecking the face of prosecutor Harvey Wilson. Judge Bowden glowered over the top of his spectacles but refrained from saying anything. He disliked theatrics in his courtroom and most of the officers of the court knew this. A look from him was usually enough to bring them back into line. In this instance it was no mystery why Wilson had resorted to shock tactics. The trial, now into the third day, had driven the jury to the brink of distraction. Wilson had a high-pitched monotonous whine of a voice. His painfully slow interrogation of expert witnesses would put a hyperactive child to sleep. But the time had now come when the judge knew Wilson wanted the jury to concentrate. Ruth Deverett was on the stand. Wilson drew himself tall, tucking thumbs into a firm hold of the lapels of his black silk gown.

"Mrs Deverett, you say you lay on the floor until you were certain your husband had left the room. How much time passed? A minute, two minutes, five minutes."

"I'm not certain. Perhaps….. five.."

Ruth Deverett's voice was barely audible. He had asked her a number of times to speak up. Wilson's head swung towards the jury. They looked attentive. His assessment was that they could hear the defendant well enough.

"What were you thinking as you lay there? Were you angry?"

A shake of Ruth's head.

"Understandable if you were."

"No. I was shaken. Frightened I suppose, but not angry."

"The anger came later?" Wilson prompted.

"No. I didn't get angry."

Wilson regarded Ruth Deverett for a few seconds. A slow shake of the head and deliberate gaze-switch to the judge. The raising of Judge Bowden's eyebrows betrayed a rare agreement with the prosecutor's intended implication: Ruth Deverett was lying.

The judge hated these trials. After all his years on the bench, the battered wives irritated him the most. He considered them stupid bitches. Why the hell didn't they just leave their men? They always stayed. They deserved everything they got as far as he was concerned.

The prosecutor's voice refocused his attention.

"Mrs Deverett. You have explained to the court how your husband allegedly brutalized you and now you tell us that this did not anger you?"

Ruth nodded, "Yes."

Wilson paused for effect. He fiddled with papers on the table - a ploy he always used to underscore a point. He would let the jurors cogitate on what they'd just heard. Spontaneous actions out of anger might be understood by a jury - even gain sympathy. But without the presence of anger any response to assault would appear more like premeditation.

Ruth Deverett had just made Wilson's job a little easier. He could feel Bowden's eyes boring into him like a slow speed dental drill. He also knew the judge had grown impatient and wanted the trial over. Delaying tactics like this would only irritate him further. However, Wilson was not about to be intimidated by any judge. He counted to five before raising his head from the sheaf of papers.

"What happened next Mrs Deverett?"

Ruth crawled out from under the table. She reached up and gripped the edging of the bench top and pulled herself off the floor. According to sounds emanating from the sitting room the news and the world kept moving on. And despite the pain, so must she. At the next commercial break Robert would expect his dinner.

Ruth took a can of beer from the fridge and placed it and a glass on Robert's special serving tray - the same one his mother had served his father's meals on. Robert liked a beer. He didn't drink a great deal, certainly not a boozer, but always a beer with his dinner.

Ruth spied the cat's bowl in the corner. She picked it up. Spatula in hand she began scooping the lasagna riddled with slivers of glass into it. After all, Wednesday was lasagna night and it wouldn't do if Robert didn't get his lasagna. The bowl filled, Ruth placed it on the tray. As an afterthought, she picked up the can of beer and shook it for a few moments. A girlish giggle bubbled in her throat. The thought of beer spraying over Robert when he opened the can drove her to the brink of hysteria. She fought to control herself. Unusual levity might alert Robert that something was amiss.

That wouldn't do.

Doffing her apron and dusting off her skirt, she noticed her pantyhose had torn. She pulled them off and dropped them to the floor. Robert didn't like snags. A loose thread on a blouse or jumper made him most unhappy. Bodily hair did as well so she shaved her legs every morning and then her pale skin that could never hold a tan. Robert detested lily white bodies. He made her cover up before she came to bed. Robert had funny ways. She would have pulled on another pair of pantyhose but didn't have time. She could hear the broadcaster announce the ad break.

Ruth picked up the tray.

Wilson saw that the jurors now hung on every word. Ruth Deverett had come out of her shell. Now she spoke clearly, forcefully. Her eyes danced, even sparkled.

"Mrs Deverett you scraped food off the floor filled with shards of broken crockery and proceeded to serve it to your husband. In a *cat's bowl*. Did you not think this might anger him, given your claim he was in the habit of beating you?"

Ruth's eyes widened.

"Oh, but you see it was Wednesday and Wednesday is lasagna night. Robert liked routine. I couldn't not serve it. That would never do. And you must understand that his usual his usual lasagna dish was broken. I explained that. "

Brows knitted, Judge Bowden looked down on her. A barely disguised waggle of the head betrayed his assessment of this woman. *The bitch is mad.* She won't leave an abusive husband and then she deliberately provokes him. God help us.

Encouraged by the judge's body language, Wilson also adopted a frown.

"And you weren't angry at any stage. You didn't scrape it off the floor cursing your husband? Rage would have been understandable."

"No. I wasn't angry."

"If you weren't angry, Mrs Deverett, can you please enlighten the court as to your emotional state?"

"Thoughtful, I think. Yes, that would best describe how I felt. Thoughtful."

"Could you expand on that a little?"

Ruth's face lost all expression for a moment. Then it brightened. Her eyes alternated between Wilson and Judge Bowden.

"I was thinking about… God. If he exists. That sort of thing. I'm not a religious person. I did go to Sunday school as a child but grew out of it. But at that moment, I began to wonder. Is there a God?"

A sharp look from Wilson to the judge.

"You were thinking about *God*. Why, Mrs Deverett? Did you blame God for what had happened to you?"

"Oh no, nothing like that. I knew the fault was mine. Robert was very convincing when it came to apportioning blame. No, I had other reasons."

"Could you be more specific?"

"Your honour." Rachel Black rose from her chair. "I fail to see any relevance in this line of questioning. Whether or not Mrs Deverett believes in God has no bearing on this case."

"I'm trying to establish the state of mind of the defendant, your honour."

Judge Bowden did not like Rachel Black. The woman had too much attitude. Her designer suits had not fooled him. Not for one moment. She had had them tailored to show the lines of her body in the most intimate of ways. Her wanton, provocative display would not score points from him. Her seductive prancing he knew was a deliberate attempt to win favour, but she was too skinny for his liking. She could look at him with those dreamy eyes all she liked; he did not find them enticing. He noted that she deliberately stood with her back to the window so that her hair glistened in the sunlight. He would order her to pin it up the next time she came into this courtroom. That would fix her. For the moment it would satisfy him not to concede her point.

I'll allow it, but wherever you're going, Mr Wilson, let's get there quickly."

Wilson's attention returned to Ruth.

"Mrs Deverett. Did you come to any conclusions on the existence of God?"

"No, and it troubled me. I mean, if someone were to die, it would be dreadful if there was nothing. You know? Just… nothing. I wouldn't wish that on anyone. Even Robert."

"I see," Wilson said slowly, adopting his special courtroom tone of empathy. "So… you had considered your husband's spiritual well-being in the afterlife. And it worried you that should he die, there would nothing for him."

"Yes. I've always been a considerate person. Robert was my husband, after all. It only stands to reason, if I needed to be considerate about a death, Robert's death would come first."

Wilson paused to give the jury time to think through what they had just heard.

Ruth stood before her husband. Without taking his eyes from the television screen he reached up to take the tray. She pulled back. Now he gave her his full attention. Again he reached and again she stepped back. Robert's quizzical expression amused Ruth. He made to rise then decided against it. Something in her manner warned him it would be best to stay seated. She stood firm as he studied her facial expression, searching for an answer and hypothesizing his next move like a soldier does when stepping through a minefield.

"What are you doing, Ruth?" he demanded, his voice not as forceful as it might have been.

"Bringing you your dinner, Robert."

She held the tray out to him. He shrank back. Refused to reach for it. Ruth let it drop. All the time her eyes fixed on Robert, piercing, belligerent. His feet splayed sideways as the bowl from the tray hit the carpet and lasagna coated his lambskin slippers.

"You fucking mad bitch. What the hell do you think you're doing?"

Ruth turned her back on him and crossed to the fireplace. She inspected the ironmongery on the brass stand and selected a heavy iron poker. She held it in both hands.

"What are you going to do with that, Ruth?" To Ruth's ears Robert's voice had a new edge. Was it fear? "T…time to stop now. Let's talk. There's no need to do anything silly."

Knuckles showed white on the hands that now gripped the armrests either side of Robert. Ruth took a step closer and smiled. She raised the poker to shoulder-height. Robert screamed and raised an arm to protect himself. Ruth swung as hard as she could. The screen of the television shattered; glass exploded across the room. She squealed with delight then turned back to Robert, her eyes tinged with insanity and glazed over with feral wildness. Robert leaped to his feet and backed around the chair. "Ruth. Please… please, calm down. Let me call the doctor."

###

"And did your husband call the doctor, Mrs Deverett?" Wilson asked.

"No, it wasn't possible. I left him and went and broke the house phone. And his mobile. It was on a charger next to the toaster. That one was harder than a normal phone. The poker didn't do much damage so I put it down the waste disposal."

Although he tried, there was no disguising Wilson's involuntary start.

"And your husband, how did he react when he saw you had destroyed his phone?"

"He tried to leave the house. But he had bolted all the doors earlier as he always did. Funny really. Robert had fitted all the doors and windows with deadlocks and bolts. He said it was to protect us from intruders but I knew it was to stop me leaving the house. Robert would lock me in before he left for work. Said it was for my own safety. I picked up the keys from the table and put them down the waste disposal as well. Robert couldn't leave. He didn't say anything. He just stared at me. I think it was the first time Robert had actually looked at me with genuine interest in many years. I suppose under different circumstances I might have been flattered."

Judge Bowden almost threw his gavel at her. *This woman is insane and the trial is a farce. She should be locked up in an asylum somewhere.*

The court clerk handed him a slip of paper. It was from his wife, Jackie. A reminder for him not to be late home. Jackie had prepared a special dinner for his birthday. He reread the, *don't be late* part. As if he needed reminding. All day he had thought of nothing else but being on time. Even after all these years, it still amazed him that he had managed to snare a former Miss West Coast winner. He remembered the early days. How he loved to run his fingers over her body. The firmness of her torso, so finely sculpted. It still excited him.

###

Ruth felt taller. Certainly the light behind her as she stood in the hallway poker in hand, cast a long shadow. She shuffled forward, her injured thigh from where Robert had kicked her causing her to limp. Robert kept his distance. *Well, why would he change now?* Ruth ruminated. He had kept his distance throughout their marriage.

She now stood before Roberts's inner sanctum.

His study.

Only Robert had a key. She had never been inside, never seen his secrets. She picked up Robert's prized golf trophy from the hall table. A statuette of a golfer on a pedestal he had won in his younger days. She had always hated it. An eyesore. It stood nearly three feet tall. Robert had kept it there because he knew it annoyed her. She stood the poker against the wall and lifted the trophy. It was heavy. The square bronzed base must have weighed ten kilos. Ruth raised it above her head and smashed it into the door. It took three blows before the locks gave and the door flew open.

She heard a gasp. A quick look over her shoulder revealed Robert had kept his distance.

She retrieved the poker and stepped inside. When she turned on the light the scene that confronted her brought her to a sudden stop. Eyebrows pressed together in a deep frown. A blink. Then another. Then a slow disbelieving scan of the interior. As Ruth stepped forward, the relevance of the contents of the room dawned on her.

And she began to laugh. No, not joyous laughter. Laughter that propelled her to her knees and slowly morphed into sobs of anguish.

The courtroom was silent. Even Judge Bowden was attentive. All eyes were now on Harvey Wilson. He knew not to savor the anticipation beyond the point of greatest impact.

"And.... what was it you saw, Mrs Deverett?"

Wilson knew what was coming. So did Rachel Black, but the jurors and Judge Bowden did not. The slightest rustle breezed through the room as they all leaned forward to hear Ruth Deverett reveal the secrets of the study.

She cleared her throat. Sipped from a glass of water.

"One wall was lined with mannequins and against the far wall there was a small table underneath a mirror with small lights round the edging. You know? Like the ones you see in theatres. It was a makeup table."

"And the mannequins?"

"Clothed in dresses. Ball gowns mostly. And on shelves behind them, wigs. I think I counted twelve. Different styles and different colours."

"Your husband was a member of the local theatre company, Mrs Deverett?"

Ruth's eyebrows disappeared into her hairline.

"Theatre? Oh no. He was a cross dresser. A transvestite." Ruth's eyes searched the jury as if to ascertain they had all understood her correctly. "Oh, but I've got to say a transvestite with….*class*. You see the clothes were of the finest quality. It seemed that even in the most perverse of states, Robert was unwavering in taste. He had always worn Italian suits and Italian shoes. Always an immaculate dresser so it was reasonable that when he dressed as a woman he would dress in the finest."

Wilson threw a sideways look at the judge then returned to Ruth.

"And how did this make you feel?"

"I was disappointed of course. Not because Robert was a transvestite but because I recognized the clothes. They were gowns I had selected when he had taken me shopping. I myself had never had such finery. Robert told me I had a good eye but lacked the flair to wear such things. To buy these gowns for me would be wasting money. Or to quote him I think he said, it'd be like casting pearls before swine. Something like that anyway."

Wilson picked up a paper from his table and gave it a quick scan.

Without looking up he asked, "What happened next, Mrs Deverett?"

"I heard noises. At first I ignored them, but the strangeness of them piqued my curiosity."

"What kind of noises?"

"It was like a bird had got trapped in the house and was trying to escape. That kind of noise."

"Where were the noises coming from?"

"I followed them back to the sitting room."

"With the poker in your hand?" Wilson asked.

"No. I had no use for it anymore."

"I see. And what did you see when you got to the sitting room?"

"Robert was hanging himself. He had put the extension power cable used for the television over a beam. The television didn't work anymore so he quite rightly found another use for it. Anyway, he had climbed onto a chair, put the noose around his neck and kicked the chair away. His legs were kicking wildly. Jerking, I suppose you'd say. And he made terrible gurgling sounds."

Wilson moved closer.

"Did you make any attempt to cut him down? Did you call the police or a neighbor?"

"Oh no. I couldn't have done that. Robert didn't like it when I interfered with his activities, but I did get a mop. Robert was urinating over the carpet and I had to keep the house clean. It would have upset Robert a great deal if I hadn't."

Judge Bowden's head was shaking. He had heard enough. This bitch had driven her husband to commit suicide. If she had left the relationship, this tragedy would never have happened. The woman's husband was a Member of Parliament, for goodness sakes. She would have known all that transvestite business becoming public knowledge would ruin him. There is no excusing her actions. She was in the wrong and he would do his best to ensure that was how the jury saw it too.

His train of thought was interrupted by Rachel Black springing to her feet.

"Your Honour. The Prosecutor has produced not one iota of evidence of criminal intent on the part of Mrs Deverett. If anything her brutalizing at the hands of Robert Deverett fully justifies a claim of diminished capacity in all matters pertaining to her husband. The available evidence establishes only one incontestable fact. From deepest shame, Robert Deverett took his own life. I ask that all charges against Ruth Deverett be dismissed. Mrs Deverett needs counseling not a courtroom."

Bowden looked at Harvey Wilson. He was not objecting to the request. He had his head down. Fiddling with papers. Wilson was weak. Bowdon had never liked him. He looked at his watch. He had a party to get to and he couldn't be late. He would delay the ruling and try to talk sense into Wilson in the morning.

"Court is adjourned until tomorrow."

"Your honour!"

"Tomorrow, Ms Black."

Judge Bowden stood and the rest of the courtroom stayed on their feet until he had left.

Harvey Wilson looked across to Rachel Black and nodded. The unsaid message was clear. He would not object to the case being thrown out.

Judge Bowden closed the front door and hung his coat on the rack behind it. A deep sigh signified to himself how glad he was the day was over. When he entered the kitchen, Jackie was standing beside the sink wiping her hands on a tea-towel.

Her eyes focused on him.

"You're late, Gerald."

Bowden checked his watch.

A chill of trepidation skittered up his spine.

"Er…only ten minutes dear. See."

A pathetic twist of his wrist so that Jackie could see the time for herself but her glare didn't leave his face.

"Late is late, Gerald."

The glint in her eye he'd seen before and come to dread. Her shape had changed since she had won the Miss West Coast Bodybuilder competition. She had become bigger.

And stronger.

She moved towards him. He froze with fear. She swung her fist. He raised an arm to protect himself but she was too strong and easily broke through his defense striking him on the side of the head. Bowden collapsed onto the floor.

He hated her.

One day he would leave the fucking bitch.

A plate smashed onto the floor beside his head covering him with pieces of cake. He knew it was carrot cake. Jackie only ever made carrot cake on his birthday.

The End

The World's Biggest Bun

The off-white walls of the lunchroom had yellowed. Kitchen ovens sat forlorn and unused. Only the stainless steel bench-top showed signs of use. Ants made tracks to a spillage of sugar and a chipped enamel jug sat in a clotting pool of milk. There were twelve tables and forty-eight chairs but only one table and two chairs showed any evidence of use. The owner had had grandiose ideas when he built his bakery in the village of Glockenspiel, but the orders from the big city never came and no more than two bakers had ever been employed.

Günter and Herman, as always, ate their lunch in silence. After five years, the two friends had said all there was to be said. Each day they ate the same lunch – sausage, cheese, and a salad of red cabbage and beetroot. When this was done, they sat back in their chairs grunting and scratching bloated beer bellies.

"I'm going to make the world's biggest bun," Herman announced.

Günter looked up from his newspaper.

"What sort of bun? Hamburger, hotdog, cinnamon, almond, sticky, plain, whole-meal? What type?"

"I don't know. What does it matter? Whatever bun I choose, it's going to be the world's biggest."

"Okay," Günter said, warming to the conversation. "Where are you going to find the world's biggest oven? Have you thought of *that*?"

"Why do I need the world's biggest oven?"

"Because, you idiot, the bun has to be baked. You won't be able to bake the world's biggest bun in an ordinary oven. If you're going to bake the world's biggest bun, you have to have the world's biggest oven. And there's more."

"There's more?"

"Sure there's more. You're going to need the world's biggest tray, for the dough."

"I'll find a tray."

"It has to fit the oven."

"It'll fit."

"And there's more."

"There's more?"

"Of course there's more, Dummkopf. You'll need to find the world's biggest hands to knead the dough, otherwise it will never rise and all you'll end up with is the world's biggest pancake."

Herman sat thoughtful for a few minutes. Then he smiled.

"That's it, then, I'll make the world's biggest pancake."

Günter kicked the sleeping dog. It yelped and leapt from the top step of the porch onto the grey paving stones. Günter stooped and straightened the doormat, then stamped mud from his boots before sitting on the bench to remove them. The dog paced back and forth, panting; its tongue drooling saliva as it solicited affection from its master. Günter grunted and the dog moved forward, but Günter glared and held up a hand.

"Stay, Belco."

Whining, Belco sat down, fidgeting and rubbing his rear end into the dirt.

Günter stomped into his home, slamming the door shut on the disappointed dog.

"Günter, is that you?"

"Who do you think it is? Of course it's me. It is *always* me."

Günter trudged through to the lounge and slumped into his chair. Rosa appeared with a stein of cold beer and carefully placed it on the small table Günter had made at night class. It wobbled and needed a wedge of cardboard to steady it. When he had brought it home Rosa had praised her husband's carpentry skills, not daring to comment that one leg was shorter than the others.

Günter was not a man to accept criticism.

He had cursed the builder of the house, calling him a son of a pig and swore that if he ever

22

saw him again he would rip the skin off his arse for making the floor uneven. He had laughed when he said this and Rosa, worn down by years of subjugation, had laughed along with him. Even so, her nerves had jangled as his beady eyes honed in on her like the sonar guidance system of a bat, seeking out morsels of reticence to pounce upon. She backed away to the sanctuary of the kitchen. Once safe, fell to one knee, crossed herself and begged God to strike her shit of a husband dead.

Rosa brought through a plate of red cabbage and liverwurst and placed it on the small table, next to the beer.

"Please don't eat too much, Günter. Your dinner is nearly ready."

Gunter held up a slice of liverwurst.

"Foolish woman. This sausage is not at fault. The meals you cook would fill any stomach. You are extravagant. It is because I give you too much money. Maybe I will cut your allowance. Then you will respect my money. You will respect *me*."

He looked up at her. She stared back, standing tall, straight backed, defiant. Then, as always, her eyes fell away. Günter sneered at the sight of her quivering lip. He hated weak women. The hookers he screwed on Friday nights would not take the crap he dished out to Rosa. Well, what did he expect? Educated women were weak. Not like the village women. Not strong like him. Not strong like a baker.

Rosa fiddled with the button on her faded paisley dress.

"How was it today, Günter? Do you have any news?"

"It is a bakery, Rosa. Why would there be news?"

"You must have talked with your friend. You and Herman sometimes have amusing conversations."

Günter smiled. He decided it would not hurt to feed his miserable wife a few scraps of humanity. After all, he was a nice guy. Everybody said so.

"There was something. Herman said he wanted to make the world's biggest bun. Can you imagine? He is such a fool, but it was an entertaining idea and filled the lunch hour."

"Really? It would need a big oven."

"That's what I said. Herman didn't think that far ahead."

"He does not have your intelligence, Günter. You must be accommodating."

"Accommodating? Do I look like a hotel?"

"I only meant that in a way it is a good idea. If he did make such a bun, he would be famous. He would be on television. Maybe they would take him to America and put him on *Oprah*. But there is only one problem with his plan."

Günter raised an eyebrow as he looked up at Rosa, his interest piqued.

"What problem?"

"I would have thought that to make the world's largest bun you would need to be the world's best baker and the world's best baker is *you*, Günter. Everybody knows that. Everyone in the village says so. They point at you in the streets. Talk about you all the time."

Günter's chest puffed out. It was true. The villagers did point at him. He saw the whispering. Now he knew why. They were in awe of him. And why shouldn't they be? Rosa, for all her many faults, did know what she was talking about sometimes. This was one of those occasions. He was a great baker, and great bakers did great things. He owed it to the world to show his greatness.

"You know, Rosa? You are right. I should make the world's biggest bun. For Herman, this is a foolish idea. But for me, not so foolish at all."

"You make me so proud, Günter."

She smiled, but her lips were compressed. Günter's tankard emptied then banged back onto the table.

"I will *do* it. I will make the world's biggest bun."

"But the oven?"

"This I will make in the backyard, out of brick, and I will fire it with wood. Just like the bakers of old. Look at this table. I made it. Is it a not a symbol of real craftsmanship? Yes, if anyone can do this, I can. Bring me another beer, Rosa, and a pen and paper. I need to make a plan."

"So do I," Rosa murmured as she hurried off to the kitchen and sought solace in the remnants of a bottle of gin.

Word that a citizen of Glockenspiel was attempting to break a world record spread throughout the town. Each morning, on a small hillock behind the iron railing fence at the rear of Günter and Rosa's house, the townsfolk gathered in ever increasing numbers to watch as Günter's brick phoenix rose from a bed of freshly laid cement.

Günter bought Rosa a new wheelbarrow.

Her job was to cart bricks to the back of the house. His, to supervise her and to build. Each day a truck unloaded wood pallets laden with bricks until the rustic-red mountain was so high that it began to look like eclipsing the house itself.

The construction was now the topic of conversation in all the village bars and cafés for many kilometers around. But, Günter's oven was taking on such a level of importance that it threatened the fragile egos of the Mayor and his town council.

A delegation from Town Hall, led by none other than the Mayor himself, stormed through Günter's front gate like a juggernaut. The fat baker was not intimidated by the diminutive figure of authority draped in the gowns of office. He ordered the Mayor and the councilors off his property. The Mayor stood firm. He demanded to see Günter's building permit. Rosa tried to reason with them. Everyone in the town liked Rosa, including the Mayor and his Councilors, but they did not like Günter and would not be dissuaded from their sworn duty to uphold town bylaws.

Fortunately for Günter making the world's biggest bun was news. Many news reporters and cameras were on hand. A reporter demanded to know if the biggest event ever in Glockenspiel history was about to be stopped. Some quick thinking was needed. The Mayor cast a nervous eye over the anxious faces of his gathered electorate then stepped up to the assemblage of microphones. Now all smiles, he assured the journalists that of course Günter had their support. And he pointed out that his name, Frankl, was spelt with no e.

When the cameras swung Günter's way, he froze like a deer caught in headlights. Instead of spouting forth words of great wisdom as he had done in the confines of his sitting room, the fat baker stood silent.

Where was Rosa? Why wasn't she here when he needed her most?

"My husband has always had high ideals," Rosa called out.

All eyes turned to the elegant woman walking towards them. Günter had to blink and refocus. Yes, it was Rosa. She wore the dress he had bought her last year when he needed her to look her best at the baker's convention. She looked like the Rosa he had first met. She moved through the crowd with the poise of a dancer. The camera on Günter switched to Rosa. She looked directly into it.

"We, all of us in this town, know that Günter Sachs is no ordinary man.

The townsfolk nodded in agreement. Indeed, none of them had ever thought of Günter as an ordinary man.

"He is a man of vision."

"*Tele*-vision, more like it," a man's voice yelled out.

A round of general laughter greeted the comment.

Günter glared, but he couldn't identify the heckler amongst the mass of faces. He turned his attention back to Rosa. She had been to a hairdresser. She had spent his hard-earned money on hair, but…. she did look good. He had to admit that much to himself. Better even than his Friday night hookers. His anger waned as he thought it through. This was perfect. After all, the baker who made the world's biggest bun would become the world's most famous baker. And the world's most famous baker deserved to have a beautiful wife didn't he? For all her faults, it could not be disputed that Rosa was attractive.

The next morning when Günter and Rosa stepped out of the house together, Rosa wore another new dress bought the previous evening. Günter had agreed that she was more use to him telling the world how great he was than toting bricks and mixing concrete. To represent the world's greatest baker she must look her best. So he'd given her money for clothes and makeup, and hired schoolboys to do the heavy work.

The crowd on the hill clapped and cheered as Rosa and Günter emerged.

Günter beamed.

The townsfolk had decided that they might as well support the asshole baker. He was bringing tourists to Glockenspiel. He was making them money.

The more commercially-minded citizens were taking advantage of the sudden glut of visitors. Frau Pushberg sent her six children and husband to stay with her sister in the capital and rented out their rooms. For the first time in many years her good-for-nothing husband and worthless children were contributing to the upkeep of the household.

The recently widowed Mrs Steiner invited two young girls from the city to stay with her. She said they were her sisters. The women of the village agreed that the sisters looked nothing like Mrs Steiner and the village busybody, Frau Brandt, remarked how odd it was that men wishing to pay their last respects would visit the Steiner house at all hours of the night.

###

Rosa continued to display the aplomb of a professional before the cameras.

"Tell us, Mrs Sachs," a journalist asked, "what made your husband decide to bake the world's biggest bun?"

Günter's mouth sagged. He shifted from one foot to the other. Was he about to be exposed as a fraud on national television? He noticed Herman staring at him. The intensity of the unspoken accusation from his workmate weakened his knees.

Rosa gestured in Günter's direction.

"Herr Sachs announced it to me one night just before dinner. Günter said he would make it his mission to bake the world's biggest bun. To stamp his mark, to make a statement that he is a great baker. The entire world needed to know that the best baker in the world is here, in Glockenspiel."

The crowd went silent. No one had imagined the eyes of the world looking on their town in such a way before, but now, after Rosa's stirring words, someone began clapping and others cheered and soon everyone was singing the village song.

Günter saw the defeated look on Herman's face.

Rosa had won the day.

An elated Günter beamed in his wife's direction. Tonight, when she brought his beer, he would tell her to pour herself a glass of wine and sit with him.

###

At the day's end Günter collapsed into his chair and reflected on his new-found status. No longer was he merely a baker; he was a television celebrity. Fame had found him just as he knew it would. Life did not get any better than this. His boss, the owner of the Glockenspiel bakery, insisted that Günter remain on full pay. Because of the publicity, the bakery had never had so many orders. Now, each morning a van load of pastries was dispatched to the city and more staff had been taken on. The bakery owner even agreed to supply all the ingredients for the world's biggest bun provided that when it was unveiled to the world, it would be known as 'The Glockenspiel Bakery's World's Biggest Bun'.

Many changes were taking place in Günter's life.

But the biggest was the transformation of Rosa Sachs.

She was more animated, exciting, and vivacious. So much so that for the first time in years on a Friday night Günter had stayed home to enjoy her company rather than visit his whores. As alcohol fueled his libido, his eyes glazed over with lustful anticipation. But Rosa held up a hand to stay his unsteady lunge at her.

"It has all been too much," Rosa sighed. "The camera lights, the crowds, the interviews,

31

your lovely wine. If I don't get some rest right now I won't be able to do you justice on the TV tomorrow. Maybe tomorrow night things will have been less hectic."

For the first time in his marriage Günter found himself alone and pining for affection just like his dog Belco.

The next day, Rosa's mother phoned to wish Günter good luck. This surprised him. When he had been courting Rosa, he'd overheard her mother say how she was foolish to ever consider marriage to such a loser and how spitting on his grave would be a waste of good saliva.

Well, who was the loser now? Not him, that was for sure.

Herman continued to protest to anyone who would listen that baking the world's biggest bun had been his idea, and really it should be he who was receiving the kudos, not Günter. No one paid any attention, especially Herman's long suffering wife who finally banned any such discussion from the house. Even his children turned against him. They'd been forced to stay home from school because the other kids had taken to teasing them that their father was mad. And they were beginning to think it was true.

So Herman, unable to stop Günter's transformation from town tyrant to town hero, fell into depression and drank beer.

###

Finally, the oven was finished.

It stood over three metres high and covered more than half of Günter's back garden. The door opening was seven metres across. It was hailed an architectural masterpiece, and the townsfolk oohed and aahed. Günter had done them proud.

In front of the oven, lying across what was left of Günter and Rosa's neatly manicured lawn, was the biggest baking tray ever made: nine metres long and six metres wide. When Rosa Googled the internet she discovered that the weight of the bun that held the existing record was more than a hundred and twenty kilograms. Günter proclaimed to the enthralled spectators that his bun would be twice or maybe three times that size. Rosa had tried to persuade her husband to be cautious with his predictions, but he refused to heed her advice.

"This is a great historical moment. The town, the media, in fact the whole world wants a bun worthy of the occasion. And I, Günter, the world's greatest baker, will give it to them."

After lengthy discussions with the owner of the Glockenspiel bakery, Günter agreed he would bake the world's biggest hot cross bun, and even better, a giant cinnamon hot cross bun. Cinnamon buns made good profit, the owner had said, and after the baking of the world's biggest such bun, and with the advent of Easter, everyone in the big city would want to buy 'Glockenspiel Cinnamon Buns'.

"Maybe we could franchise them to Starbucks," the owner had fantasized to Günter.

A surprise was that Herman suddenly stopped sulking and volunteered to help his old friend in any way possible.

"For the greater good of the village and the bakery," he'd said.

The grateful bakery owner accepted Herman's magnanimous gesture and his offer to load the ingredients for Günter's world's biggest bun onto the truck. Herman whistled the village song as he lugged sacks across the warehouse floor. He toiled with a zest and vigour seldom seen in his usual daily labours.

When the truck arrived, a line-up of helpful neighbours carried the bags of flour, the sugar, salt, cinnamon and yeast, the cartons of milk and the butter to the back of the house. A hush fell over the crowd as they watched Günter measure out his ingredients into a disused wine vat especially hired by his boss from a local vineyard and scoured clean for the purpose. Then, taking up a paddle borrowed from the local rowing club, Günter began stirring. After two hours he was done. He instructed his helpers to use plastic buckets supplied by the Glockenspiel hardware store to scoop out the contents onto the tray. Günter beat the slush with the paddle and slowly but surely the fat baker, covered in flour and looking more like "the ghost of bakers past", built a solid mountain of doughy mix.

When he stepped back to catch his breath, a stein of beer was placed in his hand. He saluted the crowd and it in a gulp. But the attention of the crowd was not on Günter. It had turned to the mountain of wobbly dough that was threatening to tip over and consume him like a raisin into a scone. A voice rose from the crowd.

"Günter just made the world's biggest dough ball."

Up went a great cheer.

Even Rosa allowed herself a smile.

Günter placed long sheets of plastic across the top of the dough then called for ladders and asked the fattest townspeople to climb atop the mound. They jumped up and down for an hour, working and shaping the doughy pile across the tray. Then, clutching their chests, the fatties rolled off, tumbling to the ground exhausted. Only the wafting aroma of hops from a trestle table covered in steins of cold beer was able to entice movement from the prostrate tubs of lard.

Günter removed the plastic sheets.

The tray was ready for the oven.

There'd been no time to build the world's biggest warmer. Günter had calculated that the conditions in the oven would be enough to make the dough rise if he left it warming a few hours longer than would normally be required. It was a risk, but the gaps between the door and the bricks needed to be sealed with a pot of cement putty to hold the heat once the oven was fired, and the cement compound needed a few hours to dry.

Günter waved forward the ten strongest men of the village to lift the tray and push it into the oven. He slammed and bolted the door shut and went to work with the cement putty.

The hour hand on his watch moved slowly.

At three in the afternoon, Günter estimated enough time had passed for the dough to rise. It was time to bake.

He struck a match and set the wood ablaze.

All eyes now focused on the gauge lodged on the left-side wall of the giant oven. The television camera lens zoomed in and a nation watched, mesmerized.

Millimeter by millimeter the needle moved upward.

When it reached the required baking heat, Günter opened the vents in the oven roof. These would be used to regulate the heat and keep the temperature even. Now all there was to do is wait.

Günter turned to the crowd.

He raised his arms in triumph, and the citizens and tourists alike cheered and clapped. Cameras broadcasting across the nation and around the world followed every move of this great man and of his momentous achievement. All were in unanimous agreement: it was a wonderful, wonderful day for Glockenspiel.

###

A hand across Herman's mouth covered his smirk.

He looked about to see if anyone noticed. The eyes of his wife were watching him. He knew the look. She was suspicious. He could see she knew he was up to something. You don't live together for as long as they had without understanding each other's idiosyncrasies.

It was time to take his leave.

Herman squeezed his way through the celebrating masses and scurried off. Once safely round the corner he rested against the wall of the bus shelter. He slapped his thigh and cackled.

"Screw you Günter. Screw you."

"What have you done?"

He shriveled at the sound of his wife's voice.

"Oh shit."

He wiped sweat from his brow. His wife leaned forward, her face inches away and her two man-sized boots planted firmly on the ground. He gulped as she placed her fists on her hips and curled her lips into a snarl, spittle settling on her chin.

"I asked you a question. What did you do?"

Herman held up his hands to fend off the blow he knew was about to be thrown. A passing villager brought a reprieve.

"Get home," she growled between clenched teeth. "We will discuss this later."

Herman nodded meekly and walked off. She would soon discover the truth. In the cellars of the Glockenspiel bakery he had found bags of out-of-date yeast. He had mixed in enough fresh yeast that Günter would not notice.

Herman detoured to the pub. When he faced his wife again and had to admit to sabotaging the world's biggest bun he wanted to be well and truly drunk.

Rosa stood in front of her bedroom mirror putting the final touches to her makeup. Her bag was packed and standing beside the bed. Every fifteen minutes, Günter, who had not stopped drinking, yelled out to her demanding his dinner. She did not bother replying. She had had enough of her pig of a husband. Her mother had been right all along: he would never amount to anything. When the time came to prove his skill as a baker, he couldn't even make a bun.

Günter watched, perplexed, as his wife descended the stairs carrying the suitcase they had bought for their honeymoon. His eyes fixated on the leather valise, then, lifting his head, he saw his wife's determined demeanor. He opened his mouth to speak but no words were forthcoming.

"I'm leaving you, Günter."

"What do you mean? I don't understand. Why? Why would you do such a thing? No, Rosa, please, you can't."

"I can and I am. The television people offered me a job and I'm taking it."

"What will I do?"

"That's the point, Günter. You will never do anything. You will never make anything of yourself. You are one of life's losers."

Rosa walked out, slamming the door behind her.

Günter stood a little unsteadily looking down at his feet. His wife was leaving him. What could he do? Then it came to him. He ran to the door and flung it open. He could just make out Rosa in the distance.

He screamed out to her, "Rosa! Rosa! I am not a loser. I made the world's biggest pancake."

The End

Nightmares

Vincent woke tangled in sheets. His t-shirt soaked in sweat.

It was the same dream, the one that had haunted him every night for a week. The images were unnerving in their clarity. And the face of the woman so familiar now he would recognize her on a crowded street. Each morning her screams would snap him out of his slumber and left him gasping for breath.

He sat on the side of the bed and lit up a cigarette. Stared down at his feet.

The woman's face continued to haunt him - trapped in a psyche that refused to abandon her to the mists of forgetfulness like all other dreams. As in preceding days, he knew the woman's face would stay with him for hours. But what truly gnawed at him was that her killer continued to remain in the shadows.

A chill breeze gusted through the open window. He reached for the duvet that had fallen to the floor and wrapped it round his shoulders. Whiskey dregs floating on the bottom of the glass on the bedside table caught his eye. He sipped the remains. There was just enough liquid to wet his tongue. Not enough to feed the craving, quell the headache or soothe a hangover. And he had all three.

Holding the duvet in place, he walked through to the sitting room. Unsteady fingers twirled the cap off the bottle he took from the cabinet. One swig to his mouth and a double shot into his glass.

He crossed the room and eased onto the chair in front of desk.

The forefinger of his right hand hovered above the keypad as if trying to find its bearings. He let it fall on the enter tab. When the screen-saver disappeared the raw mocking truth revealed itself; there were no additions to the 'Chapter One' typed some days ago.

Jeremy, his agent, would be disappointed. Pissed off, more likely.

The publisher was crapping all over him. Screaming for the second novel they'd paid an advance for. Now they were threatening to sue Jeremy if a manuscript was not forthcoming. It interested Vincent they would sue the agent and not the writer. He worried for Jeremy, but what could be done? Writer's block happened to all authors didn't it?

But this was not simply writer's block, this was different. The dreams made it different. Then there was Cassandra. Without her he had no muse. It was she who had given his life purpose. Whiskey had now become a substitute. But as much as he drank to forget, he could not forget. His future was trapped in the past. He could see no way forward. He lacked the will to move on, to stop the slide.

A need for caffeine drew his bare feet to the kitchen. He flicked the switch on the kettle then extracted a mug from the heap of dishes stacked in the sink. He rinsed it under the tap and wiped it clean with a dirty tea towel plucked from under a pile of empty pizza cartons. The woman in his dream had a nice face. A gentle grace to her movements.

Not unlike Cassandra.

Was that it? Was he trying to replace his lost love? He thought for a moment. But no. The dream woman possessed a reality quite distinct from any other woman he'd ever known. Every instinct in him said she existed in the real world.

He poured hot water into the cup - two thirds only. The rest of the way he filled with whiskey. He carried the mug through to the dining table and slumped into a chair. The smoldering stub of the last cigarette lit a fresh one. Another indifferent start to what he knew was going to be a long and depressingly non-productive day.

Vincent finished his coffee and sipped on a second glass of whiskey. It had gone nine thirty.

He scratched at his stubble. He needed a shave and a shower but lethargy was proving master over such mundane needs. He stumbled across to the settee, turned, and fell backwards.

It started as a light tap then grew louder and louder.

Vincent tried to ignore the sounds, drifting back into his inebriated coma. The banging continued to a veritable frenzy. His eyes blinked open and he stared at the door.

It would have to be Jeremy.

Not a friend. They'd all abandoned him. As had his family. He was beyond redemption, he'd been told.

"How do you save a drowning man who won't reach for the life preserver?" his sister had screamed at him before slamming the door.

Well, what did he care? He had Jeremy. Not that Jeremy was really a friend. In fact, he was pretty certain Jeremy didn't really like him very much at all. But Jeremy brought him money. And the money bought whiskey.

Vincent struggled to his feet and opened the door.

"You look like shit," Jeremy said as he barged in. "Have you had any sleep?" He walked across to the computer and looked at the screen. He spun round. "For God's sake, Vincent!"

Vincent reached for the bottle and refilled his glass. "Nice suit Jeremy. What is it? Armani?"

Jeremy shook his head in disgust. "You need a haircut." He sniffed the air, "And a shower."

Vincent shrugged and sank onto a chair at the table.

"You're taking advantage of me, Vincent. Abusing my trust. All right, all right. You're the best talent I've had in a long time. I just hate to see it go down the toilet, that's all." Jeremy's anger waned to frustration, then to defeat. He dropped onto the seat opposite Vincent.

Vincent watched the metamorphosis. He had seen it before. Every second day in fact.

"I'm having the dreams again, Jeremy."

"Cassandra is dead."

"This is another woman."

Jeremy looked at him.

"Jesus, Vincent."

"Another woman, Jeremy. Another woman and it's the same killer. There's a fucking serial killer out there. It's screwing with my head. I can't concentrate."

"Maybe you should stop drinking."

Vincent glared and Jeremy raised his hands as a peace gesture.

"All right Vincent, tell me about the dream."

"I'm inside an apartment. I don't know where it is and I don't recognize the woman, only that she is in her late twenties. The same age as Cassandra. Attractive. Short dark hair. Anyway, she's just finished showering and is walking into her bedroom, naked, drying her hair. There is a television in the room. The news is on and she stops to look at an item. The killer is hiding in the wardrobe. I can't see his face. He grabs her. Throws her onto the bed. She is screaming. Thrashing about. Then I wake."

Jeremy rubbed his forehead.

"You write murder mysteries, Vincent. You could be dreaming up a plotline or maybe subconsciously you're having these dreams because you want to save someone from Cassandra's killer. Maybe that's why you don't recognize this woman as someone you know. You need to save someone, anyone, because you feel you need to redeem yourself somehow."

"Don't you think I've thought of that? No. This woman is real, I know it. I don't want more blood on my hands."

"That's stupid talk, Vincent. You know that. It's not your fault Cassandra died. The police wouldn't listen when you went to them. But how could you blame them? There was no evidence only a dream of a man killing your fiancée. Not even a description. You couldn't save her, Vincent. This is misplaced guilt. How many times must we have this conversation?"

"I could have warned her."

Jeremy nodded, "Yes. You could have warned her."

Vincent waited but Jeremy had nothing more to say. The discussion was over. Vincent hated that. He wanted to argue the point. He needed to argue the point. They had gone to the police together. The police had thought he was mad. They had convinced him not to tell Cassandra for fear she might turn into a nutcase, living each day looking over her shoulder. Not on evidence as flimsy as his nightmares.

He had yielded to their rationale and then what.

Cassandra had lost her life, that's what. And in the circumstances he had dreamed she would. The police said it was a dreadful coincidence but a coincidence all the same.

Jeremy checked his watch.

"I have to go. You need to do some work. Write about your dreams. Change it later, but if that's all you can think of right now, begin there."

"Maybe you're right." Vincent decided Jeremy deserved a few crumbs of hope. "Maybe it's some sort of creative message. I'll start writing up that sequence and see where it takes me."

"Good man."

Jeremy gave Vincent a reassuring pat on the shoulder and let himself out.

Vincent downed the rest of the whiskey then collapsed back onto the settee.

###

Buildings float by. The city street he recognizes but the name of it escapes him. He centers on the café drifting into focus ahead. Tables line the pavement surrounded by flowers. Lots of flowers. The reds, blues, whites, pinks pulsate in time with his own quickening heartbeat. The woman is there, sitting at the only table with seats. Dressed in white. The satin glistens in the sunlight. She looks towards him. Smiles. Beckons. He's being pulled towards her. Now the flowers are changing colour. Bright red. The stems wrap around him, clinging, like vines. Tugging at him. Slowing him. A man is behind her. He sees Vincent's struggle. Laughs. Vincent wants to scream a warning to the woman. His mouth is open but there is no sound. Then he sees the name above the café doorway: Le Brie.

The whiskey glass lay on its side. The contents spilt across the carpet.

This time the dream was more surreal than real, but the images, still vivid. He had seen the café name. He knew the place. He'd eaten there.

And that the woman had been sitting in the full light of day meant she was there for lunch.

Vincent's eyes sought the clock. Eleven.

He rolled upright with sudden determination. Today, Le Brie was where he would go for lunch. The decision had been easy but dealing with a swimming head was not. Vincent swayed as he made his way to the sink and filled a glass with cold water. Two effervescent vitamin B tablets went in. When they'd stopped fizzing he gulped the mixture down. Shaking his head did not achieve the level of focus he had hoped for.

But if he could brace himself against a cold shower, that might work.

Vincent sat at an outside table that afforded him the best view of the entrance to La Brie. Unlike in the dream there were no flowers on the tables. Only a glass bowl filled with sachets of sugar and sugar substitutes. He ordered chicken salad and iced water, the healthy food a necessity and the water to clear his head but it did not moisten his mouth. It still felt as if a bucket of sand had been poured into it.

He mulled over his earlier conversation with Jeremy. Maybe his agent was right. Writing about a writer with writer's block who dreams of women being murdered by a serial killer did have potential. Especially when one of the victims was his former lover.

The lover he had failed to protect.

The story could track the writer's desperate attempt to uncover the identity of the next victim. Not only to save her, but to trap the killer into the bargain. Yes, he thought. Not bad. That does work. Now that the creative processes had kicked in, Vincent's mind darted in a dozen directions. He ordered a cheese platter, more iced water and a coffee. Ideas began to take shape across the pages of his notebook. The dam had broken. He knew how it would go from here on. Once he started on an idea he always managed to work it through to the end. Each concept triggered another. It had always been like that for him. By morning the storyline would be complete.

As the waiter refilled his coffee, he saw her.

The wind flicked at her hair. Designer clothes clung to her lithe body. He was looking at beauty and elegance. She chatted and laughed with the two women walking beside her. Vincent liked the look of her. An enchantress, if he were to write her praises. The trio took a table inside but from where he sat he could clearly see her through the open window. His head began to spin. He took deep a breath. Calmed himself.

What now?

She gazed in his direction. For a moment their eyes locked. It could have been just one of those arbitrary eye-contacts with strangers that occur every day. But her startled reaction surprised him. Recognition? Surely not. Then her gaze shifted. He had seen that type of look many times. She knew the face but not from where. He was a celebrity, after all. A long time had passed since his last book but he had made many television appearances, been featured in newspapers and countless magazines. He had grown used to being not quite recognized.

He thought about telling her straight out of the danger threatening her. He was half-way to his feet before common sense intervened. She would have every reason think he was a nutter. Maybe call the police on him. No. He would watch over her for the time being and decide later what to do.

Vincent sat and Jeremy paced.

"Unbelievable, Vincent. You tailed the woman all afternoon then followed her home. It's called stalking. You could be arrested."

"Okay. What else am I supposed to do? She's in danger."

Jeremy halted and fixed his eyes on Vincent. "It was a dream *dammit*. What if she isn't in danger? You had a dream, that's all. You believe it's real and that's it, nothing more."

"Don't forget the first one," Vincent said.

"All of this could be your subconscious," Jeremy said. "You believed you dreamed Cassandra was murdered and then it happened as you believed it would. The dream could have been a coincidence. It happens all the time. Read the papers."

"No! That is not how it was."

"Will you at least consider the possibility?"

"I know what I saw, Jeremy. How else would I know this woman? Answer me that? I'd never seen her before until today. She came to the restaurant in my dream and today, at the restaurant, there she was. I recognized her immediately. Explain that."

"Maybe you went looking for the woman in your dreams and found a close resemblance. Jesus, Vincent, I don't know."

"It's her," Vincent said, but with less conviction. He was willing to concede Jeremy might have a point. He would not say it out loud. Jesus, what if Jeremy *was* right. Was he losing his mind?

"Vincent all I'm asking is slow down. Think about it before you do anything silly and we all end up in jail."

Vincent nodded. Then smiled.

"Good story though."

Jeremy grinned. "You've started writing?"

"The first chapter, halfway through the second," Vincent lied. His steady eye contact with Jeremy would have fooled a priest. "You were right. It's an inspiring turn of events. Right after you left this morning the words began to flow."

"Well then, I take everything back. If it keeps you writing, do whatever you want. I'll put aside some bail money, just in case."

That surreal floating again. Inside her apartment. She is checking her answerphone. A quick shake of the head. No messages. A jug of water in hand she waters the pot plants. They sit on a rack just inside the door to the sitting room. The empty jug goes onto the table. Chores finished, she undresses as she walks. He savours the sensuous unveiling. Her body is firm. Tanned. A beauty. When she's naked, she walks into her bedroom and on into the bathroom. He can make out her shape through the steamed-up shower door. She returns to her bedroom, toweling her hair. The towel cast aside she falls across the bed. Eyes closed her right hand touches her breast. A gentle fondle, nothing more. Slowly it moves down her body. Vincent floats closer. He wants to be near her. Share the erotic moment.

Loud ticking disturbs his concentration.

The clock on the bedside table. His eyes swivel to it for just a second.

Almost midnight.

Eyes back to the woman. Face aglow, her eyes remain closed. She is lost in another world with a fantasy lover.

A shadow falls across her. Vincent screams a warning. And jolts awake.

In the dream she had been dressed as Vincent had seen her earlier in the day. Something fluttery began in his innards. The clock on the bedside table had shown midnight. Did this mean her murder would take place tonight? He checked his watch. It was almost eleven. What to do?

Should he telephone Jeremy? Or the police?

What was the point?

He threw on a pair of jeans and a sweatshirt. It occurred to him he had no idea of the build of the murderer. He had not seen him clearly enough. What if, physically, he was too big to handle. He needed an edge. He took the breadknife from the sink, wiped it dry, wrapped it in a tea-towel then thrust it into his belt. His sweatshirt easily covered the protrusion. He gave a final thought to phoning the police then dismissed it. If they went to the apartment now and saw nothing they would conclude he was an idiot and by morning the girl would dead. After what happened to Cassandra, he would never be able to live with himself not if it happened again.

He would prevent the murder and worry about the consequences later.

Vincent parked down a side street two blocks from her apartment.

A still night. Clear sky.

It was twenty minutes to twelve. Enough time.

He crossed onto her street and moved along the tree line until he was opposite her ground floor windows. For the next few minutes he waited. Observed. Where would the killer be right now? He had to be nearby. Then he remembered the dream. The girl wandered about the apartment before going into the bedroom.

The killer must already be in there somewhere.

Vincent gulped back the sick sensation rising in his throat and steadied himself against a tree trunk. Eyes scanned the windows. Most of the lights were on. He caught glimpses of her moving about in the kitchen and lounge. Not in the bedroom yet. That had to be good.

He crossed the road and slipped down the side of the building, stopping at the first window. It was dark inside. A spare room? The window easily opened. Was this how the killer had entered? Was he inside this room, waiting in the darkness?

Vincent unwrapped the knife and held it in his hand. If the killer attacked as he climbed in, he would be ready. He leapt up and flung his leg over the sill. A heave and he was in and on the floor, knife at the ready.

The door burst open.

Light blinded him.

Vincent froze, like a possum caught in headlights. The woman in his dream stood in the doorway. A shotgun in her arms aimed directly at him. Her knuckles white on the trigger guard.

Detective Sullivan knelt next to the body. He held the piece of paper at arm's length and compared it to Vincent's face, ignoring the shocked look and vacant eyes.

"What do you think, Gil?" Frank Sullivan asked his partner.

Gil Landy said, "I think that I don't know anymore. It's identical. How spooky is that."

Frank rose with a nod and brushed the dust off his trouser legs.

"Weird. All the details exactly as Cheryl Reems described. The artist's sketch of our killer could not have been more accurate. The whole business floors me."

"And we never believed her," Gil said. "He broke in through the window just as she said he would. The knife on the floor is exactly as she described. He was preparing to kill Ms Reems like she dreamed he would. Nightmares, she called them. But accurate down to the last detail."

"A premonition. I've read about it. Never seen it happen until now."

"Well, whatever it was, the fact she dreamt this guy was stalking her and knew when he would make his move saved her life. She didn't have a licence for the shotgun. It's her father's. Do we charge her with unlawful possession?"

Frank shook his head.

"No way. The woman told us she was going to be attacked. Even the date. And we ignored it. She had to protect herself because we wouldn't. The press would crucify us. Both of us would spend the rest of our careers teaching children how to use pedestrian crossings. It was self- defence and we'll leave it at that."

Gil shrugged his shoulders. What did he care?

The man in the shadows across the street watched as a body bag on a gurney was wheeled to the ambulance. Sure he felt cheated but he was still alive. The bitch was walking about with a shotgun. If that idiot hadn't climbed in through the window, it might be him in the body bag. It was her lucky day. He would find someone else.

There was always someone else.

The End

The Artist

Eight am. Time to get up. Claire's legs swung over the side of the bed. Arms dropped to rest across her thighs. Today she turned forty. She glanced across at the shape stirring beneath the silk sheets. She smiled. Her lover and partner completed her. And tonight, Jack was throwing her a party.

At forty it was time to reflect. There was much to celebrate. Happiness. Success. A secure future. Her life had turned out much better than she had dared dream.

She pushed herself off the bed. The slap of bare feet on timber floor took her to the bathroom.

Teeth newly brushed. A gargle of mouthwash and then an inspection of eyes and lips for tell-tale signs of lines. She found none. The investment in lotions and facials was paying dividends. Did she look forty? The image looking back at her still looked pretty good. No fat. Hardly any cellulite to speak of.

But those forty years. They had passed so quickly.

And how different it might have all turned out.

At an early age she had wanted to be an artist. To paint a great masterpiece. Have her work hung in the world's most famous galleries. An uncompromising and uncharitable art teacher shattered the dream. He took great delight in informing her parents that she was incapable of drawing a straight line, let alone something as complex as a circle.

Claire's doting parents dedicated themselves to uncovering the talent they knew their daughter possessed. DNA on both sides had produced musicians, artists, writers and even a potter of sorts. Whatever talent Claire had lurking beneath the surface, they were intent on finding it.

Music came next. Firstly the piano. Then the guitar. Lastly a school recorder, which also proved to be the last straw. The monotonous musical form of Chinese water torture disappeared after two nights.

Accepting Claire's deafness to all tone, her parents dragged her through the portals of dance schools. At last one kindly tutor said it was best not to spend money on lessons when it was obvious her feet were more suited to a sports field than ballet.

Pottery classes turned out unusable ashtrays and sewing lessons unwearable dresses.

Claire turned on the shower and held her hand under the cascading water until the temperature suited her. She let her toweling robe slide to the floor and stepped in.

She couldn't remember if those early failures had depressed her. She didn't think so. Not buoyed as she was by her parents' optimism that discovery was only a matter of time.

When it came, it was more a gradual realization than a lightning bolt.

Claire learned that her talent was that she could see talent in others. Could distinguish between what the market might accept as gifted and reject as mediocrity. How rewarding this had proven.

Lifting her face into the steaming rivulets of water Claire allowed herself a congratulatory smile. She owned a gallery and represented the country's leading painters and ceramics designers. Each year she held exhibitions in the major centres. And corporate clients readily trusted Claire's judgment that the artworks she selected for them were a secure investment. Over the years the value of the paintings supplied by her had consistently appreciated well beyond expectation.

She was the best in the business.

She stepped out of the shower and reached for a towel.

But if she had not met Jack….

###

In her early days as a budding dealer, enthusiasm waned to despondency as Claire learned the harsh lesson that the art scene was far more competitive than she had imagined. Being new to the business was difficult enough, but being deemed too young to be taken seriously by the creative fraternity was an almost insurmountable obstacle. Established artists gratefully accepted the free dinners and listened politely to her sales spiel as she explained why she should represent them. But by the time they were sloshing down the third bottle of over-priced wine it was clear they were keen to get into bed with her but for sex, not business.

She had nothing to offer the artists, no gallery of her own and with limited finances that was not likely to change in the near future. But she had a work ethic. Sweat and calloused hands didn't frighten Claire. She devised a business plan of sorts. But mostly she knew that her pathway to success was going to be a hard slog and it would mean dedicating her life to her work.

Claire had always been a social animal and most of her friends were well off and therefore potential customers. She accepted every invitation to dinners and parties that came her way. She never intruded her paintings into conversations, but whenever asked about her work she took the opportunity to mention she was happy to deliver collections for relaxed home appraisal.

Painstakingly, Claire built a base of suppliers. Mostly fringe artists that other dealers were not interested in, but sales were made and the rent was paid. After working long hours each night, she would return to her empty apartment and empty bed. Before she drifted off into a restless slumber she'd question if the sacrifice was worth it. In the beginning her response was always "yes", but as each year passed she wondered how much longer she could continue eking out a living before she ceased to believe the lie.

Then came the day that changed her life forever.

Claire first heard of Jack Loxley through one of her clients. The client had kept a brochure from a Loxley exhibition. He liked Jack's work and wanted to buy more to hang in the foyers of his expanding chain of corporate offices. The client, Claire knew had a discerning eye and if he thought Jack Loxley's work was worth that type of investment then it must be so. Intrigued, she made some calls.

It was confirmed to Claire, by the owner of the gallery that last exhibited Jack Loxley's work, that he was indeed a talented painter. But he little understanding of the commercial realities of the art world and had displayed no desire to learn or to co-operate. He was independently wealthy so the selling of his work was not critical to him. When Loxley had agreed to an exhibition, the gallery worked hard to ensure a successful night. They discussed with him how he might best present himself. They explained to him he had a crucial role to play in the sales process.

But Loxley displayed scant concern. He drank too much, abused patrons and assaulted one important buyer. The gallery washed its hands of him and when news of his behaviour spread, no one else wanted a bar of him. He faded from the scene.

The gallery owner had not been seen or heard of him for a couple of years.

Perseverance paid off. Claire tracked him to a studio in the Waitakere Ranges.

Her information was he had become a recluse. Claire suspected it might be more a case that if the world did not want Jack Loxley, then so be it. He had shut himself away to sulk. She was becoming attuned to the eccentricities of artists. Most were temperamental and needed kid-glove treatment. And when it was needed, Claire could do kid glove.

She stood to make a lot of money if she could secure Jack Loxley's paintings for her client. Enough to open her own gallery. No sulking artist was going to stand between her and her dream.

The driveway wound its way up through a forest of native trees and ferns to a multi-level natural wood home hidden from the road. Tyres scrunched loose metal as Claire drove across an unsealed turn-round before parking under the bough of an old Kauri.

Three steps led her onto a cedar deck. She knocked three times. A few minutes passed. No reply. A quick scrutiny revealed a pathway running down the side of the house. Claire decided to follow it. Ferns flicked at the legs of her navy slacks and when she reached the clearing at the back of the house she spent a few moments removing seed heads imbedded in the weave of the fabric.

The studio stood detached from the house and precariously poised a few metres back from the cliff edge. The view across the forested valleys to the ocean took Claire's breath away. An inspirational panorama were her initial thoughts.

She picked her way across a line of slate slabs to a glass paneled door. Muffled sounds of a gravelly-voiced Leonard Cohen came from within. She did not bother knocking. The tapping would never be heard above the music.

The door was ajar. She pushed it open.

Jack Loxley stood in the centre of the room, piercing grey staring directly at her.

Claire found herself looking at a man with the physique of a swimmer. His six foot frame was clad in denims, track shoes and a black t-shirt. Long jet black hair fell just short of his shoulders. Tanned and handsome, he looked more like an Italian movie star than the obnoxious malcontent she had been led to believe he was.

Loxley waved her inside and pointed to a table positioned next to a floor-to-ceiling window.

The studio was much roomier than it had looked outside. Tall timber-paneled walls bore many paintings. More lay in piles on the floor. Jack Loxley's talent was inescapable. His style unique. Claire knew she was looking at a collection of great value.

She sat on one of the two chairs and looked through the window. With no solid ground features for reference the building could have been floating in space, and the voice of Leonard Cohen some disaffected angel. It occurred to her that any artist would be inspired to creativity in such a setting.

Loxley took a bottle of Chardonnay from a small fridge in the corner. He pulled the cork then brought the bottle and two glasses to the table. He sat, filled the glasses then pushed one towards her. They sipped the wine in silence. The music stayed loud and Claire decided that whatever game was being played, she would play along.

When the bottle emptied, Claire stood. She placed her business card in front of Loxley and left.

Whatever it was that had taken place, Claire's gut told her Jack Loxley would make contact. She prayed to God he would. They had to work together. He was a great talent and he had enough finished work for a number of exhibitions. He was attractive and that would go down well with buyers.

Talented and handsome. A winning combination.

###

Over the next week Jack Loxley was uppermost in Claire's thoughts. By the end of the second week there had still been no contact. She felt herself becoming increasingly anxious but along with the nervousness an increased sense she must wait him out. All her instincts told her he would call.

It was late Friday afternoon at the end of the third week when the sounds of stampeding horses came from her mobile phone. She tapped the answer icon.

"What do you want from me?"

She recognized Jacks voice.

"I want to sell your paintings, to be your agent. You need to be seen, Jack."

She held her breath. Not daring to speak. The silence was excruciating but she was experienced enough to know not to force him.

"I agree," he said. "It's been too long. Come to the studio on Monday."

The phone went dead.

Claire leapt from her chair and squealed with delight.

###

She rented premises for a week in the city centre. Close to a parking building. Nothing turned clients off attending an inner city exhibition faster than a lack of parking. No one wanted to walk any great distance, not these days.

She well knew that in her line of business presentation was as important as the art itself. And next to hanging spaces, the most important part of presentation lay in the framing. She contracted the best framer in town and convinced him to make the trek to Jack's studio.

As the exhibition day drew near and the days turned into nights, Claire and Jack spent a great deal of time together. As they became more comfortable with each other, the conversation flowed, and an endless supply of Chardonnay kept glasses filled, yet despite the ever-increasing consumption of wine and their developing relationship, he had not tried to seduce her. She mulled over the idea that maybe he might not find her attractive. She had a nice figure and exercised to stay in shape. Friends said she was good looking, and she thought she was as well.

To Claire's surprise the real reason for his lack of interest was revealed at the end of the second week.

When she heard the unaccustomed sound of heels on the pavers outside, she stopped what she was doing and focused on the door. She was so used to the idea that no one ever came to the studio the footsteps had startled her. She glanced across at Jack but he was disinterested and did not bother to look up.

A wreath of smiles appeared at the door.

"Hi guys."

One of the most beautiful women Claire had ever seen stepped inside. She was a genuine tall, leggy, shoulder-length-haired blonde bombshell.

"Claire. This is my wife, Gillian. Gillian, this is Claire."

Jack made no effort to raise his head.

"Jack. The tone of your voice. A little enthusiasm, please, hello Claire," Gillian said.

Claire, shocked, confused, taken aback, mouth open, reached out and shook the offered hand.

"I can see Jack hadn't mentioned he had a wife, Claire. Well he has and here I am." She emphasized the statement by pointing to herself. "Now, what do you think of Jack's dabbling? Is there a living here, do you think? I keep trying to convince him to get a real job. But Jack is Jack. He has to find himself. Boys will be boys."

Jack said nothing. He focused on trying to match one of the various types of framing to the painting he was holding. Claire finally remembered to close her mouth. She picked up a canvas, studied it, then carried it across to the table. Gillian followed chatting away, seemingly impervious to Jack indifference. The obvious friction between the two made Claire uncomfortable. As she half listened to Gillian, she kept an eye on Jack. He ignored both of them.

The exhibition was a huge success. Claire then took Jack's art to all the major cities of the North Island. Each canvas sold for many hundreds of dollars more than expected. His self-imposed exile meant his earlier transgression had fallen off the public radar. He was seen as a new and exciting talent and buyers couldn't get enough of him.

Over the next three months Claire travelled and had little contact with Jack. She wanted him to work. Produce more paintings. They were making a lot of money, and long may it continue. More importantly she had engaged a real estate agent to lease premises on Ponsonby Road.

Her dream of a gallery was about to become a reality.

And Jack's paintings would guarantee her future.

Her success with Jack spread throughout the art community and established painters began to make contact, asking her to represent them. She considered that at this rate she might need to employ staff.

When she returned to Auckland she tried to make contact with Jack. After a few days of no response she drove out to the house. She found him in the studio sitting at the window. Two empty Chardonnay bottles sat on the table, and a third bottle sat half empty.

He didn't acknowledge that he had heard Claire enter but she knew he knew she was there. She looked about the studio. The walls and floor were empty. A knot formed in her stomach. But before she had gathered the wit to say anything, Gillian walked in behind her. The Norse beauty had dressed in a tight black satin pants suit that she must have been poured into. It showed her body to perfection and Claire could see how Jack might be besotted with her, even to tortuous distraction. But there was something else going on here. Jack's gazing out the window appeared to be quite adrift from reality.

"Claire, how wonderful to see you," Gillian sparkled with her usual chirpiness. "As you can see the studio is emptied of those smelly paints. I've convinced Jack to turn it into a guest house. Such a wonderful view. A waste not to make use of it don't you think?"

It would appear Jack's hard man image did not apply to Gillian. He was a blithering mess caught by a black widow spider, and the longer the nightmare continued, the more entangled he would become in her web. Claire knew Gillian's type. She would break into tears anytime Jack broached the subject of his unhappiness. What a manipulative bitch. Right then Claire wished she had a mallet so she could drive a wooden stake through Gillian's heart.

Claire brooded. Despair turned to depression. Finally, when felt she had reached rock bottom, feral instincts took control and logic devolved to cunning. A plan formulated. After all, she reasoned, was it not her job to keep her client happy and Jack was far from happy.

She sent a message asking Jack to meet her at the gallery. When he arrived she marched him down the street to an Italian restaurant. When the meals came Jack ate but Claire pushed at her pasta with a fork.

Jack watched her. Bemused yet intrigued.

"What's on your mind Claire?"

Looking about to ensure other patrons were not listening she leaned forward.

"She has to go, Jack. Gillian. She has to go. You have to get rid of her."

Jack found a dot on the table and focused on it.

"You have to tell her the marriage is over," Claire went on. "You are a wonderful artist. A great talent. You're not working. She is making you unhappy. That's not a marriage. Not in anyone's book."

Jack's eyes rose.

"You're serious," he said.

"Very serious. She has to go and that's an end to it."

Claire held his eye. She was determined not to look away. The waiter interrupted the optical showdown but she sensed a victory when she saw Jack was nodding as the waiter filled their glasses.

"You're right Claire," Jack sighed. "But you have to understand. Gillian is a wonderful person. You've seen the worst of her but she isn't always like that. She just doesn't see art as a profession. To her it's a hobby. Why she wants to be with me I've no idea. She would have been much happier with a lawyer or an accountant. She wants her man to wear nice suits and take her out to dinner. She was a model, a social animal, and I'm not. Chalk and cheese. I wish it was different but she's not the sort of woman you can leave on the shelf, is she?"

"No, she isn't," Claire responded.

"But you're right," Jack said. "Painting is my life. I'll do it."

But Jack procrastinated.

Weeks went by and nothing happened.

In the end Claire stepped in. She began by lunching with Gillian on a regular basis under the ruse of developing a friendship for Jacks sake. Lunches morphed into theatre openings and dinners. Claire ensured that Gillian and Jack's relationship became a constant topic of conversation. She planted seeds of discontent. And having developed fertile ground she kept planting.

When Gillian announced the marriage was over, Jack had mixed feelings. He was sad to have lost his wife but exhilarated that he could now fully focus on what he loved most and that was his art. He promised Claire he would keep her gallery full and was true to his word. Without the constraints of the demanding Gillian he found his way once more and produced his finest works.

It was in that year that the tradition of Jack throwing a party to celebrate Claire's birthday began. He always booked out one of the city's best restaurants and ensured all her friends and her better-known clients attended. It was always a wonderful night and she was eternally grateful.

And today was her birthday and she was forty. Tonight was her party and she was looking forward to it as she always did. Life didn't get much better, she thought. She had money, success and a partner she was very much in love with. Her life was truly complete. She looked down at the naked outline beneath the sheet. She affectionately reached across and stroked the exposed thigh. She heard a sigh and the bed creaked as she watched her lover turn and look up at her.

"Happy birthday," Gillian whispered.

"Thank you," Claire whispered back.

No, life did not get much better. She had Jack's art and she had Jack's blonde bombshell.

The End

The Dementia Man

At 4:30pm traffic slowed to a crawl. Exhaust fumes blanketed by an atmosphere of ninety percent humidity generated a noxious irritating cloud that made the old man cough. Unsteady, a rush of displaced air in the wake of a passing bus sent him reeling backwards. He managed to reach out and grab hold of a parking meter and stop himself falling. Asthmatic gasps hunched his shoulders and he stayed bent in half until his breathing recovered. Stronger, he returned to the spot he had occupied all morning. There, he fell into shuffling back and forth, all the time eyes fixed on his sandals and his unclipped fingernails scratched at his head of grey hair.

The old man had come to the attention of Sanjeev Singh when he'd opened his dairy at 7:30am and refilled the cold drinks fridge near the door. Sanjeev concluded from the man's unkempt appearance that he was homeless and this obvious sign of deprivation meant he was probably hungry. Throughout the day Sanjeev remained vigilant. He would be ready if the homeless man tried to steal from the display stand by the door. But the old man never came near the shop. He just stayed on the corner, walking back and forth. The day had been long and he was tired. Soon his wife would relieve him. He would go home and lie on the couch and watch the last hour of cricket. Still, he would warn his wife to keep an eye on him.

When Sanjeev's wife, Ava, arrived, she did not see what her husband had seen. Instead, she saw a frightened old man. Someone lost, disorientated, confused. She telephoned the police.

Matt Bronson jiggled the handle to make sure the lock had caught, then removed the key. His shift now over, it was off to the refuge of the gym. In an hour he was meeting his brother-in-law Larry at the Irish tavern. Tonight was the Rugby League Semi-Final between the Warriors and Manly. Neither he nor Larry had cable television so whenever the Warriors played they went to watch the games on the tavern's big screen. As he grabbed his sports bag he caught his reflection in the locker room mirror. Straightening, he patted where his t-shirt pulled tight across his abs. Firm and hard. The women that passed through his life said he looked good without a shirt. The extra ten minutes added to his workouts had done the trick. His trainer had told him abs were sexy, and he had been right.

"Not bad for forty," Matt said, giving them a last pat.

"Sarge. Got a minute."

"Not now, Jacobs. I'm finished. Take your troubles to Roberts. He's duty sergeant now."

"I can't find him."

Jessica Jacobs reminded Bronson of a startled sparrow. She had a permanent nervous look and an earnestness that irritated the hell out of him. He also didn't like it that she was a loner. He had tried to get on with her, invited her for drinks, but Jacobs was no mixer. The word in the department was that she wasn't into men, probably gay. He believed it. It would explain why she chose her own company over a night out with his six-pack abs.

He had scanned her records. When she was eleven her father had run out on her and her mother. A lucky break for Mum it seemed. The records showed Dad had been arrested on a number of occasions for beating her up. He supposed it went some way to explaining Jessica's attitude to men. The home would definitely have become an anti-male domain with a mother passing on her bitterness to the next generation.

Matt made to brush by her.

"Go stand by his desk. He'll turn up."

Jacobs stood her ground. "Sarge, this is important. I know the difference. I wouldn't bother you otherwise."

"You have a minute to convince me." He held up his watch for her to see. "Go."

The young constable took a deep breath as if about to run a hundred meter dash.

"One of the cars brought in somebody. He had been bothering the shopkeepers on Jervois Road. At first I thought he was another homeless man. I had a doctor check him out. He has dementia, Alzheimer's disease."

"I know what dementia is, Jacobs. Get on with it. You have thirty seconds left."

"We checked through his pockets. No ID, nothing. Just a note wrapped round a door hinge. The note said, and I quote, 'I am being held captive, they will kill me in forty-eight hours, please get the police'."

Jacobs stood and waited. Matt watched her watching him. She reminded him of a hawk eyeing its prey before it swooped. She was not about to let him get away. He rubbed his forehead. She had him and they both knew it.

"Fuck, fuck, fuck, fuck, fuck." Matt unlocked his locker door and threw his bag back inside then slammed it shut. Jacobs flinched but didn't move. "Okay, Jacobs. Now that you've completely fucked my evening, take me to this man and this fucking note."

"Listen up," Matt said as he entered the meeting room.

Twenty minutes had passed. He had taken the note to his superior and was promptly put in charge of the follow up. He had not bothered to change back into uniform. Even if he missed the gym, he still had hopes of making the game. He left a message with his sister to inform her husband he might be late.

"Time is against us on this one. I want it dealt with quickly."

The two constables and detective assigned him sat with pens poised.

"Our John Doe is a Caucasian male. Approximate age, seventy years. Found standing on the intersection of Jervois and Ardmore. The doctor has confirmed he has dementia. He has no idea who he is or where he came from. No ID. For the moment we will refer to him as Mr Smith. Mr Smith had a note in his pocket." Matt held up a photocopy. "The note says that someone is being held captive, they will be killed in forty-eight hours and to bring the police. Unfortunately, Mr Smith has forgotten where the note came from. Bad luck for the victim."

A hand went up. Matt shook his head at the detective.

"Question time in a minute, Larry. Now, this note might be bogus but for the moment we treat it seriously. This means urgency. We need to know who Mr Smith is. We have no reports of a missing person as yet, so he hasn't been missed by loved ones. But, given his condition, he must be in somebody's care somewhere. Larry, you check with the Alzheimer's Society. Get the names of all local specialists. He was walking so let's presume Mr Smith lives nearby. Jacobs, you and Gerry take a photo and get a description out to the media. I want it on the next news bulletins. Questions? "

Larry decided against it.

"Good. Okay people, let's move. We meet back here in one hour."

The rapid tap of Matt's pencil on the table was the only sign of his mood. He glanced up at the clock. The football game was underway. Mr Smith sat, elbows on the table, resting his head in his hands. Jessica Jacobs re-entered the room, whispered into Matt's ear then sat next to the old man. A gentle hand fell on his forearm.

Side on she had a nice profile Matt thought. Fine lines.

"Mr Smith, we have news for you. Your son is here," Jessica said.

"My son?" The old man wrung his hands and shook his head. "I'm sorry. I don't remember a son. I'm such a nuisance. You have been so kind. I feel so useless. I'm so sorry."

Jessica looked across at Matt. He shrugged but said nothing. He checked his watch. His night might be saved after all.

There was a knock on the door. A constable popped his head in.

"Sarge."

Matt got up from the table and followed the constable from the room.

"Tell me Gerry?"

"Sarge, this is Frank Horgan, Mr Smith's son. Mr Smith's real name is Arthur Horgan."

Arthur Horgan's son was a big man, overweight, not muscled. His clothes didn't quite fit; they made him look uncomfortable. The buttons of his checked shirt threatened to fly off and expose a beer barrel belly. A swatch of thinning hair unsuccessfully attempted to cover a balding head. Matt didn't like the look of him. He had an intolerance of anyone out of shape. How difficult could it be to exercise?

"Mr Horgan. Thank you for coming so quickly," Matt said. "I have a few questions. You have ID?"

"Already checked it, Sarge," Gerry cut in. "Driver's licence and passport and a family photo clearly showing Mr Smith, um, Horgan."

"Good. We found a note in your father's pocket. It said someone was being held captive and was going to be killed if the police did not rescue them. We think your father in his wanderings has been given the note. Now he can't remember where he got it from."

"My father has dementia. He imagines many scenarios because he never knows who he is or where he is. He writes notes all the time."

Matt held up the photocopy of the note.

"And does this look like one of his notes?"

Frank Horgan leaned forward and gave it a quick scan.

"I can't say for certain but it's highly likely. As I said, he lives in a fantasy world."

Matt flicked the photocopy with his fingers. He made a decision. "Excuse me for a moment."

Matt walked back into the interview room.

"Mr Smith." Matt was not about to call him by any other name. Not yet anyway. "Here is a pen and paper. I want you to write 'Please bring the police'."

Arthur looked puzzled.

"Go ahead," nodded Jessica.

Arthur gave her a cursory glance and she smiled encouragement. He wrote on the piece of paper as instructed. When he was finished Matt put the two documents together.

"Jesus fucking Christ."

Disappointed groans greeted Matt as he entered the Bar. A quick glance at the giant screen covering half a wall showed the Warriors were losing by ten points. Typical. He'd raced for nothing. He looked over the heads of the gathered masses until he spied his brother-in-law. He bought two beers and made his way towards him.

"Hey Matt, you made it," Danny said. "We have company."

"Hi Matt."

It was Matt's sister.

"Danny, you brought your wife. You know the rules. No women on football night."

"She's your sister. You tell her."

"Matt, this is Bronwyn from work," his sister said.

Nice smile and nice body. Matt put the two beers on the table and held out his hand. Bronwyn held on a little longer than necessary. Susie gave him a conspiratorial look and Matt clicked immediately: another blind date. Still, Bronwyn was not bad looking. Better than some of the others she'd tried to set him up with. The crowd moaned. Matt looked up at the screen. The Warriors had fallen further behind.

Matt was losing interest in his team and turned his attention to Bronwyn. For the next twenty minutes they traded information about each other's private lives. Bronwyn was an accountant. She had been married but no children. She liked sports and had even run a marathon. Matt found himself warming to her and was already thinking of the night ahead.

Bronwyn was distracted by something over Matt's shoulder.

"I think that woman over there is trying to catch your attention," she said.

Matt looked to where she was pointing. "Jesus Christ."

It was Jessica Jacobs.

"A girlfriend?"

"No, a work colleague."

Bronwyn gave him an 'I'm not sure I believe you' look.

"It's work, I promise. Excuse me a moment."

When Matt reached Jessica he took her arm and guided her into the foyer.

"Out with it, Jacobs. Why are you here? What can't wait until morning? And how the hell did you know where I was? "

Jessica's eyebrows raised.

"Everyone on the force knows you come here when the Warriors are playing, Sarge. I wasn't happy with tonight's outcome. I'm not certain sending Arthur home was the right thing to do."

Matt took a moment to calm his irritation. Much as he considered Jacobs a pest of sorts on duty, Jacobs out of uniform was not quite the Jacobs in uniform. Tight jeans and T-shirt suited her way better on her than the shapeless police blues. She wasn't bad looking he supposed. However, her mood was far from sexy. Right now she looked like a pit bull waiting to rip his throat out.

The crowd inside roared. The Warriors must have scored.

"Okay Jacobs. Tell me why."

"Call it a hunch or whatever but I didn't like the look of Arthur Horgan's son. I thought maybe he might be abusing the old man in some way. You know it happens. I ran a background check on him. Nothing came up so I checked everything including births and deaths."

"What the fuck for?" Matt said, exasperated. The sound from the crowd inside was now bordering on hysteria. "He's the man's son. He had ID to prove it. And without wanting to sound callous, why the hell would he want to claim an old man with dementia if they didn't belong together?"

"That's the question I'd been asking myself," Jessica said. She took a document from her pocket. "But the bigger question to ask is how was it possible that Frank Horgan was able to take his dad home tonight when records clearly show his father died in a car accident seven years ago."

Jessica handed Matt a copy of the death certificate. Matt scanned it then read it through again. He raised his head. Jessica nodded when she saw Matt comprehend.

Another roar from the crowd. Matt looked towards the bar.

"Fuck, fuck and double fuck."

The glass paneled door rattled from a none-too-gentle rapping from Matt's knuckles. When he and Jacobs left the tavern the Warriors had drawn level. This bloody investigation meant he would miss the most exciting, in fact, the *only* exciting game of the season. He stamped both feet as he waited for the door to be answered. He scowled at Jessica. It irritated Matt that she ignored his disrespect and returned a tolerant smile, or was it a smirk? Was the bitch patronizing him? He banged on the door again. A piece of loose putty fell onto the welcome mat.

"Pass me that pot plant," Matt snapped, pointing to the small terracotta pot a metre to her left.

"You can't break in, Sarge. We need a search warrant."

"Jacobs, are you certain of your information?"

She nodded.

"Then pass me that fucking pot plant."

He was not about to show deference, legally mandated or otherwise, to the man forcing him to miss the football. Jessica held out the pot. Matt snatched it from her hand and used it to smash a glass panel. Shards of glass tinkled across the floor inside.

"No carpets," Matt observed.

He reached through the jagged opening and unlocked the door. A light went on in the next house. A curtain pulled across. "Nosey fucking neighbours. That's all we need. Stay right behind me Jacobs," Matt ordered as he entered.

He opened the first door along the corridor. His hand snaked around the door jamb and felt for the light switch.

"Bingo."

Matt switched on the light.

Just inside the door a table. Scattered across the table and all over the floor were empty plastic water bottles and sheets of paper with numbers scribbled across them. The window on the far wall had been padlocked shut. Above it a smaller a window gaped half open. In the centre of the room sat a single bed. A chain had been looped through the iron frame and on the end of the chain a set of handcuffs. The handcuffs were clamped to the ankle of Arthur Horgan. His head rested at an unnatural angle on the mattress. In death, his lifeless eyes managed an accusatory stare.

Matt knelt and checked for a pulse. He looked up at Jacobs and shook his head.

"He's dead."

The smell of urine and excrement was overpowering.

"Where the hell is that smell coming from?" Matt pulled out a tissue and covered his nose.

Jessica lifted a sack draped over a small waste paper bin in the corner.

"The toilet," she said, staring down at the uncovered bucket. She dry retched, dropped the sack and turned away.

Matt passed her one of his tissues.

"Come on. Let's get out of here and secure the rest of the house."

The next room looked to be an office. Used coffee cups sat on the desk. A number of floor boards had been pulled up. Matt and Jessica peered into the hole. It held a floor safe with the door open. Matt rubbed the back of his neck, the Warrior's game now well and truly forgotten.

"You better call it in, Jacobs," Matt said, his tone softer, conciliatory.

"I'll do it outside if you don't mind, Sarge. I need some fresh air."

"Sure. Go ahead. I'll check the rest of the house."

Five minutes later he joined Jessica outside. "There's a spare bedroom in the rear of the house. There's some mail on the bed, addressed to Frank Horgan. It's pretty obvious what happened here. Horgan was a boarder and he found out about the old man's safe. He's been trying to get the poor old bastard to remember the combination. Tonight he got lucky."

"Looks like it, Sarge. Then he killed him, cleaned out the safe and scarpered."

Matt said, "By the look of the number of sheets of paper lying about, it's taken a long time for him to remember. It must have been the visit to the station that jogged his memory. What beats me is how the old bugger managed to escape in the first place. Guess we'll never know."

"At least we know who the killer is. It's something, at least," Jessica said. The note the old man wrote. He must have thought that when he had the chance he would throw it from the top window. Then just forgot he had it."

"Dementia is a shit of a disease," Matt said.

Jessica walked away to meet the arriving patrol car.

Matt thought through his actions. Had the football game distracted him? Would he have checked as Jessica Jacobs had done if he had not been distracted? She was a good cop, even if she was a cold bitch and a man hater. She came through with a result. He would write her efforts up in his report. She deserved a pat on the back.

Matt was thankful he had joined an all-night gym. Exercise cleared his head and he needed to erase images of the old man from his thoughts. He worked his routine harder than usual. After half an hour he was gasping for breath. Beads of sweat rolled down his face and across his abs.

Jessica, too, perspired. She too pushed her body to its limits. Her sweat-drenched t-shirt clung to her breasts like a second skin. Her nipples, easily visible through the flimsy material might have been tantalizingly erotic to a voyeur hiding in the trees, watching. But Jessica was confident she was alone.

She paused to catch her breath.

Matt Bronson, the egotistical chauvinist asshole, had surprised her. He was going to put in a good word on her behalf. It would go on her record that she had carried on with the investigation and it was because of her diligence they had found the body. He would not mention she had dragged him out of the tavern and neither would she say anything. After all, they were colleagues, and colleagues supported each other. But she knew Matt's momentary lapse into benevolence would be as long-lasting as an ice cube on an oven hot-plate. In the end he was a man and all men were the same.

She had seen the way he looked at her, ogled her. If she let him bed her, afterwards he would toss her aside like a dirty sock into a laundry basket. Gossip was he did that with all his women. All men were the same. They disgusted her.

She stopped digging. The hole was deep enough. She dropped the spade and walked to her car and opened the boot. Frank Horgan looked up at her. The eyes on the fat man were wide with fear, confused. She helped him climb out. His hands, handcuffed behind his back, made movement awkward. He grunted and screamed but the crumpled rag she had shoved into his mouth muffled the sound.

Jessica pointed in the direction of the hole. Horgan's head made rapid shaking movements. She reached into the boot and pulled out a tyre lever. As her captive cringed from her she swung the lever at the side of his head, enough to stun him.

"Come on Frankie. Let's just walk. Don't make this any more difficult than it needs to be."

Frank Horgan shuffled forward on unsteady legs. He recoiled in horror as he recognized the shape of the yawning hole now at his feet.

Jessica smiled.

"That's right Frankie. You don't mind if I call you Frankie, do you." She swung the lever into his knee. He dropped to the ground. "Sorry. I know you're probably thinking there's no need for that but I think you might get it into your head to make a run for it and I can't have that, can I? I could easily lose you in this bush."

He whimpered. He looked up. Eyes pleading.

But Jessica was not about to spare any sympathy on Mr Smith's murderer.

###

From the start, and unlike Matt, Jessica had been suspicious of the man calling himself Mr Smith's son. The old man had been gentle and the son was an asshole. She could not accept they might be related and decided to check the son out. When she uncovered his deceit, she had gone to the address given by Horgan when his ID was checked at the station.

The door had been ajar.

Inside she heard shouting. A voice she recognized as Mr Smith's begged to be left alone. Deciding there was not time to call for back up, Jessica pushed through the door and crept along the hall. Horgan was kicking Mr Smith, demanding he give up the numbers. Mr Smith, chained to the bed, was unable to crawl away. He tried to fend off the blows but his arms were weakening and Horgan's boots were getting through his guard and striking his face.

Jessica looked on in horror.

Then memories from her past exploded into her head. She was eleven again. The images so clear, it was as if it was yesterday. She had come home from school to find her cocker spaniel was tied to the washing-line pole. Her father was beating him with a golf club. Jessica remembered Goldie's yelps of pain. Goldie, her only really true friend. Whenever her mother was beaten, Jessica always ran to her room and climbed under the bed and held onto Goldie for dear life, waiting for her mother's cries to stop. Now her sadistic father was doing it to her dog. She ran to the tool shed and snatched up a hammer. Her father did not hear her come up behind him. She kept hitting on his head until her mother pulled her away.

Now, as Frank Horgan beat the old man, she only saw her father. She crept up behind and hit him hard behind the ear with her baton. And, like her father, he collapsed in a heap. She cuffed him then looked to help Mr Smith. The old man lay still. Jessica took his wrist and felt for a pulse. Nothing. He was dead.

She quickly checked the rest of the house. In the second room she saw the hole in the floor and the safe.

At the station she had gathered up Arthur's doodling and shoved the papers into her pocket.

For some reason she had kept them when she changed out of uniform. Like the papers scattered about the floor, the writing on the papers she now held consisted of numbers. One set of numbers had been circled. She knelt on the floor and dialed them into the combination. The door opened. After a rough count, she estimated the wads of money amounted to more than five hundred thousand dollars. She put the money into a paper bag and tossed it into the boot of the car. With some difficulty she managed heave a now semi-conscious Horgan into the boot after it. After stuffing a rag in his mouth and whacking him back into a coma she went to the Irish Tavern to look for Matt Bronson.

Satisfied Mr Smith's killer was immobile, Jessica bent down and removed the handcuffs. Hands free, Horgan tried to crawl away. Each painful movement brought a whimper. Jessica struck him on the back of the neck and he lay motionless. She then rolled him into the hole. He groaned and lifted an arm. She picked up the shovel and swung it, hitting him again and again.

It took an hour to fill in the hole. She patted down the dirt and covered it with leaves and brush. No one would find the grave. Very few people came to this part of the West Coast. There were 'No trespassing' signs all over the bush-covered property, a gift from her abusive father to her mother for keeping her mouth shut, and now, finally, from her mother to her.

It would never be sold, nor would she ever live on it. She would need to be careful how she spent the money. Her home needed renovations and new furniture would be nice. Maybe she would take a trip. Then she would set about laundering the money into investments. Her stint in the fraud unit had taught her some useful lessons.

Maybe, if Matt Bronson decided to vent his spleen on her again or started treating her like shit in any way, she might invite him out here for a picnic. He would jump at the chance.

Jessica threw the shovel and cuffs into the boot. No one would ever find Frank Horgan or her father.

Nor would they find the others.

The End.

The Affair

The white paint on the ceiling had yellowed. Cigarette smoke or neglect take your pick. The curtains needed a wash. The sparsely furnished room needed dusting. But Ellen did not care that the motel was sleazy. The sheets were clean and the bed was comfortable. Little else mattered. The sex had been so exhilarating. Every cell in her body had bubbled and spat static like aluminum foil in a microwave oven.

Today, Ricardo had taken their sexual journey to new heights. A level of ecstasy she had never dreamed possible. She had feared her racing heart might burst from her chest. Now, she lay on her back gasping air waiting for her breathing to steady to a slow rhythmical pant.

To Ricardo she was just a slut and he treated her like one. She didn't mind. She loved every minute of it. She loved when he talked filthy to her and she loved talking filthy back. It was icing on their climactic cake.

Why couldn't Larry be more like this?

Her husband was the antithesis of Ricardo. Larry was a gentle, man, with the emphasis on gentle. He treated her like a rose petal when she craved to be yanked from the ground like an obstinate weed.

Ricardo filled the gap. Her Italian stud; all looks and arrogance and as shallow as a saucer of cat's milk. There was no depth to Ricardo, no deep conversations. He was a pleasure giver and this he did with the expertise of a Casanova. Around his neck, gold plated medallions dangled on the ends of cheap imitation silver chains. Ricardo looked more like a hooker's pimp than the Italian movie star he imagined himself to be. The balding head and burgeoning beer-belly added a final touch of the slovenly. Ricardo encapsulated the depth of degradation she had allowed herself to sink to. And, she loved it.

Within these walls Ricardo was her walk on the wild side.

At home Larry was her normal.

From time to time she reflected on the two men in her life. Both were of the same age and physique. But there the similarities ended. How was it she could be attracted to such complete opposites?

A deep sigh left her lips. The midday liaison had drained her. How she would love to close her eyes now and sleep. Just a short nap. But it was time to leave. Ellen stretched then turned her head towards Ricardo. As always he lay on his side head on hand, watching her, ogling her nakedness. She fought the urge to pull a sheet across. Her shameless exhibitionism actually thrilled her. Brought a blush of pink to her cheeks.

But the real world tugged at her conscience. She had children.

A twist and a roll and her feet met the floor. She took a clean pair of panties from her purse and before she disappeared into the bathroom she struck a final naked pose to tease Ricardo.

She was still giggling like a naughty schoolgirl when she stepped under the shower.

Ellen stopped off at the supermarket. The kids would be home from school within the hour and the cupboards were bare. The thought of grumbling teenagers was more than she could bear. Also, in her haste to meet Ricardo she hadn't taken anything out of the freezer for dinner. She resisted the urge to settle for takeaways, the usual Friday night treat. The kids might ask what's up.

As she reached for a tray of lamb chops in the meat section she caught her reflection in the mirror.

She was aglow.

An attempt to stifle a laugh resulted in a snort. A quick look around. No one looked in her direction. What if the children noticed? She should join a gym. Then she would have a reason for looking like she had just run a marathon.

The sound of the television met her when she walked into the house. She checked her watch. The kids had beaten her home. She dropped the shopping on the bench and turned to the sitting room door.

"Have you kids done your homework?" She yelled.

"Where've you been?" Her son's voice came back at her. "I'm hungry."

"At the supermarket. Got caught up in traffic, and if you can't feed yourself then you can starve."

"There was no food."

Ellen smiled. Breathed a sigh of relief. They wouldn't move until dinner and that suited her. She put the groceries away and went into the laundry and dumped the panties from her purse into the laundry basket. She didn't need the kids finding them in her handbag and asking awkward questions.

In the bedroom she stripped. Did a quick pirouette in front of the mirror. Pretty good shape for a woman of forty with two teenage kids. At least Ricardo thought so. She moved closer and studied her face. Some crow's feet round the eyes but otherwise no lines. Her mother had insisted she stay out of the sun when she was younger. How right she'd been.

Through the years her brunette hair had gone through various stages of length. Never more so than now.

Larry liked it short.

"Be neat and prim and tidy," he would tell her. "Look your age. Nothing worse than mutton dressed as lamb."

Ricardo liked long hair. He wanted to hold onto something when they romped about the room. Recently she had let it grow. As yet Larry hadn't said anything. She may yet have to ask her hairdresser for a compromise solution.

Ellen threw on a mauve tracksuit and went back down to the kitchen. For the next twenty minutes she put her afternoon liaison out of her mind and concentrated on preparing dinner. While pots bubbled on the range-top she placed cutlery beside the table mats. She intended feeding the kids first, and eat with Larry later. He was working late. She always waited for him when he worked late.

It seemed she'd had quite a few late dinners recently. She didn't complain. Once she had commented that surely a law firm as big as the one he worked for had partners that could share the workload. Larry gave her a grimace of a smile, shrugged, and went back to reading the paper.

He never really talked about his work. He knew she found it dull. And it was. When Larry chose to become a lawyer, it was not as a litigator or even property law. No. He chose a tax consultancy. In Ellen's book tax consultants ranked alongside accountants and the security guards that stood outside banks as the world's most boring jobs.

Sometimes over coffee with friends Ellen would listen as they discussed conversations they had had with their husbands. She always changed the subject when eyes turned her way. Debating changes to tax law was not her idea of a fun evening and certainly not a subject she would relate to her friends.

Nowadays, she and Larry hardly talked at all.

He would take his paper through to the sitting room and peruse it as he watched television over the top of the pages. She would immerse herself in a book. Not that she minded so much anymore. It was relaxing. Her trysts with Ricardo more than satisfied her needs for sexual release and companionship.

She had an ideal life, and long may it last.

Sally was thirteen going on thirty and John was fifteen. Where Sally was observant, curious and naturally suspicious, John was docile, non-caring and egotistical to the point of narcissism. He was interested in girls, not siblings. He tolerated Sally and her friends, and although he had to admit a couple of her friends did catch his eye, they were still only thirteen. For much of the time he mostly ignored his sister.

When Sally told him their mother was acting strangely he dismissed it for two reasons. One, he wasn't interested and two, he *really* wasn't interested.

"Parents always act strangely, that's the world they live in," he'd said.

Sally pouted and stormed off to her bedroom.

But she was not to be put off.

During dinner she watched her mother's every move. When her father commented on Ellen's buoyant mood and her mother turned away crimson-faced, Sally had no doubts something was up. She recognized a mask of guilt when she saw it. She had seen enough of them on television. Oh yes, there was something going on and Sally was determined to get to the bottom of it.

She glared at John, trying to catch his attention. He was too busy filling his face to have noticed anything. With a sigh she accepted her role as detective; a lone private eye.

Over the next few days, whenever Sally was home she stalked her mother. However, a daughter so readily available did have consequences. Sally found herself washing dishes and hanging washing on the line. Brother John, oblivious to her sleuthing efforts, sat in his room listening to music and playing games on his computer

On the third day Sally gained reward for her perseverance.

She was sitting on the Persian mat; the one that once lined the hallway but was now hidden behind the settee because of the hole the cat scratched in it. The morning's chore was to straighten books on the lower shelf of the bookcase. The phone rang. Just as she made to get up her mother answered it. After a normal greeting her mother's voice dropped to a whisper. This served to alert Sally something was up. She crawled to the end of the settee and peeped round the mahogany leg. The muscles at the bottom of her neck tensed when she saw her mother look around nervously like a bag lady guarding a stolen supermarket trolley full of aluminum cans. Her mother held a hand across her mouth as she spoke into the phone.

Sally held her breath.

"I can't, the kids are home," she heard her mother say. "What would I tell them?"

Sally sucked on her thumb to stop herself from making a sound.

"Okay. I'll give them some money for the movies. Give me an hour."

When her mother put the phone down and disappeared into the kitchen, Sally hurried off to John's room.

Ellen parked. Checked her makeup in the rear vision mirror. Applied a touch of lipstick then climbed out of the car and made her way across to room sixteen. There was a spring to her step. She was a bounding antelope leaping across the veldt in search of its mate. If she was a peacock she would have preened. Her faced beamed sexual signals like cheap Las Vegas neon lights. If the motel manager saw her he would know what was up. But she didn't care. A wild afternoon awaited.

She didn't knock. Just flung open the door. An arm reached out, took her wrist and pulled her inside. She squealed in protest but the sound was cut short to the outside world as the door slammed behind her.

"Now do you believe me?" Sally demanded, hands on hips.

"I believe you. Jeez. But what do we do?" John said.

"We have to confront her. It's the only way."

"You're mad. We can't do that. Besides maybe the guy in there is much bigger than me. He might lose his temper."

Sally thought this over. It had never occurred to her there might be violence.

"Just as I thought," John said, sensing triumph. "You hadn't thought that far through, had you?"

"It doesn't matter. Mum wouldn't let anything happen to us."

"Look Sally, I know you think you're doing the right thing but what is it you hope to achieve? Do we tell Dad?"

"Of course not. I just want Mum to stop whatever it is she's doing."

"But that's it. I mean, what is it she's doing? We don't know for sure. It could be something completely different to what you think. Maybe she's helping the police with undercover work. Maybe this is a secret rendezvous with her handler." Sally looked confused. "I mean, how certain are you she is having an affair and not something else?"

"I can't say for certain."

"There you go. I think it best we go away."

"No way," Sally said. "We need to at least look through the window."

"And how do you propose we do that? We can't just bowl up to the window in broad daylight. Someone might see us."

"We go round back. Where we can't be seen."

Ellen lay naked, spread-eagled, her wrists and feet tied to the four corners of the bed. Ricardo had blindfolded her and had been massaging her with a glove made of opossum fur. The touch was ticklish and at the same time arousing. She purred like a cat. He threw the glove to the floor and took up the whip made of lengths of felt. No matter how hard he hit it would never hurt, not even if Ellen had been a butterfly.

He removed the blindfold. Ellen played her role to perfection. She looked up at him in feigned horror.

"Are you going to obey me, you slut."

"Never, you asshole. Let me go."

Ellen struggled but her restraints held her. Ricardo swung the whip.

"Let me go. No please. You're hurting me," Ellen cried.

"You deserve it. Say you deserve it."

"No. Never."

"Say you're a slut."

"Let me go, I'll never talk."

Ellen's arousal heightened by the second. Heat invaded her head as she neared her peak. She knew that at the moment she begged him to, Ricardo would throw himself upon her. But delaying her own gratification always made their inevitable congress so much more delicious when it happened.

Sally found a fruit crate by the rubbish bins. John carried it across and put it under the bathroom window. She climbed up.

"Oh my God," Sally whispered. "Mum is tied to the bed. Someone is beating her."

"Let me see."

John climbed up and after a minute he jumped down.

"Maybe she really is working undercover and they've found out," Sally said.

"She's crying for help. He's hurting her. Hell, what do we do?"

"Phone Dad," Sally said.

John hand produced his mobile. He speed dialed his father's work number but couldn't get through to him...

"Shit. A recorded message. Dad's in a meeting. Come on, let's go find someone who can help."

Ellen's libido levels had climbed like mercury in a barometer and threatened to explode through the top of her head. She could bear it no longer.

"Now Ricardo. Now! I'm a slut! I'm a slut! Take me."

Ricardo freed her hands and legs. He climbed onto the bed beside her and leaned forward kissing her neck.

"For God's sake, Ricardo. I don't need foreplay. Just bloody get on with it."

Sally and John rushed into the motel office. John pressed his thumb down on the buzzer button embedded in the counter top and held it there.

"Alright, alright I'm coming," a voice called from the back. The man who stepped through the curtained door towered over the two teenagers. He was overweight and waddled as he walked. A stained purple T-shirt desperately tried to cover his pot belly.

"What can I do for you two?" He grunted.

He was huge and that was enough for Sally.

"You have to help us," she said. "Our mother is in trouble."

The motel manager scratched his unshaven face and looked at Sally and John as if they were aliens. "She is in one of your motel rooms. A man has her tied up and is beating her."

"She's working undercover for the police," John added.

"Which room?"

"Sixteen."

The manager reached behind him and took a key from a rack on the wall, "You kids stay here."

"No way," Sally said. "We're coming too."

"Well, stay back, out of my way. Got it?" he scowled.

Two nods.

###

Ellen was reaching her climax. Ricardo egging her on. Sweat dribbled from his chest onto her face. She didn't care. She wanted to taste his sweat. The excitement and intensity of this moment of passion was crashing through new boundaries. She had never experienced such ecstasy. They had climbed a mighty mountain. Now they had reached the peak.

"Mum!"

Somewhere in the deep recesses of Ellen's mind she heard the call.

"Mum!"

The voice was softer. Not Ricardo's. His thrusting had stopped. Then the weight was gone from atop of her. She flung her arms to the side. Exhausted, but frustrated that she had not exploded as she had expected to. She opened her eyes. Searching for Ricardo. Why had he stopped? She saw faces looking down at her.

At first, comprehension evaded her. Then realization dawned.

"Noooo…!" Ellen screamed as she reached for a sheet.

"Mum, what's going on?" Sally cried. "Dad, what are you doing here? What are you doing to Mum?"

John turned away in disgust. Ellen continued to wail.

Months passed before Ellen, Larry, John and Sally returned to a semblance of normality. A psychologist had counseled the children through the trauma of seeing their parents copulating. Helped them understand that adults sometimes role-played to add spice to their sex lives. It was healthy. Sally was not convinced and asked a local Catholic priest what steps she needed to take to become a nun. John went back to eating and his computer.

Sadly, Ellen acknowledged her relationship with her children was now different. Instead of simply ignoring her, as they had in the past, they now ignored her standoffishly. The shocked looks on Sally's and John's faces continued to haunt her. She had not made love to Larry since the day in the motel.

But as the weeks passed the fretting waned and deviant thoughts began to return. After six months she longed for Larry's alter ego Ricardo to reappear.

One morning Ellen heard a noise over the sound of the vacuum cleaner. It seemed a hundred horses were galloping across her driveway. Turning off the appliance she went in search of the cause.

Outside was the largest motorcycle she had ever seen.

Dressed in black leathers and legs astride the rumbling engine sat Larry, both hands gripping the handle grips. His right hand rolled the throttle back and forth. The revving was deafening. He smiled and turned the engine off.

"Larry, what the hell is this?"

"I don't know any Larry. On the road I'm called Bear. I need a biker bitch to go riding with. I'm told I might find one at this address."

Ellen's eyes lit up.

"Well, hello Bear. Let me go in the house and get her. Don't you go anywhere." Ellen rushed inside wondering if she could still fit into her jeans. What did it matter? She had a pretty good idea of what Bear's taste in a woman's dress sense would be.

The tighter, the better.

The End

Mending Kittens

I stayed out of sight and watched from the tree line.

Alicia would not have liked this day. No sun. She loved the sun. Said the rays cleansed her. Like having a shower without water.

"The rays kill the bacteria," she'd said.

I'd shaken an unbelieving head.

But today, on the one day that was Alicia's special day, sorrowful heads of battleship-gray clouds hung low robbing the world of colour. The flashes of lightning were drawing closer but the rain held off. It seemed that not even God was about to shed tears over a tortured soul lost to Him long ago.

No family members at the graveside. No friends. Only a policeman and a female clerk from Social Welfare, both there as a public service acknowledgement that Alicia Bunning's begrudging presence in government departments had ended. Her, now to be closed file would doubtless discover more ready acceptance in the archival crypt.

The government lady, fifty-ish, bespectacled, blue and silver streaks through light brown hair, glanced up at the overweight cop. She said something. He laughed. Almost a snigger. She checked her watch. Turned her wrist to the cop. He nodded. Alicia had taken up too much of their valuable time.

My attention turned to the priest. The man of God clutched a tattered *Book of Common Prayer*, a papery prop that would have been held aloft through many sermons to ever diminishing congregations. His knuckles gleamed white in response to the falling temperatures. He whispered a prayer of eternal rest then touched the casket lid.

Two men in luminous orange vests stepped forward and lowered Alicia's plain coffin into the cold, muddied hole. Even before the small gathering of indifferent mourners had turned to leave, the graveyard employees had bent to shoveling the sod. Perhaps their haste was in fear that the approaching storm might collapse the walls of Alicia's place of interment. Perhaps it was just disrespect for a young woman of little substance who had died before her time.

Fingers of light played with my eyelids. I resisted being wrenched from slumber. An aching head needed rest. But a dry mouth demanded water. I had suffered a sleep deprived night due to the incessant buzzing of a mosquito above my ear. Now, my surroundings awash with dawns early light I held out the back of my hand. The greedy little creature, more interested in blood than safety, settled. I slapped and wiped the bloodied residue onto my jeans.

Yawning, I stretched then sat up. Fingernails rasped through the growth on the side of my face. It had gotten longer. I could almost twirl the scraggy ends between thumb and forefinger. Officially a beard now I supposed. I fell back onto my bed of cardboard spread over the grass. Droplets of water splashed onto my face and drew my attention to the darkening heavens.

I needed to move.

Grabbing the sack that held my meagre belongings, I leapt over the 'Do not walk on grass' sign and ran across the manicured lawns. I paused on the sidewalk and waited for a road sweeper to crawl past me. Whirling brushes swept up plastic bottles, paper, and probably a few used condoms. Two hookers, mascara seeping from the corners of their eyes, sipped on take-away coffees at the bus-stop. The night people were heading home and day workers not yet filtering in to replace them.

Rain droplets now spotted the pavement with increasing rapidity. I stepped off the kerb and made a beeline for a canvas canopy protecting the doorway of a menswear store. I would wait out the heavy rainfall. Keeping dry a priority. I hated begging for money in wet clothes.

Mocking me from the shop window was the reflection of a thin, haggard creature of jaundiced complexion. It caused me the same twinge of horror that I had seen many times reflected in the faces of passers-by. Disgust from the general public for an unhealthy specimen doomed to have his face on police posters and disease advisory booklets.

The family doctor had described me as suffering from excessive consumption disorder, a kinder way of informing my parents their son was a junkie and an alcoholic. Righteous conscience mandated that they should waste inordinate amounts of money on quacks. There would be no miraculous cure, the doctors had said. In other words, just leave him with us and keep sending cheques.

My first incarceration was in a New Age health clinic hidden away behind two-metre-high hedges in the revamped buildings of an abandoned school. We inmates spent our days listening to waffle and sitting on wooden benches in the shade of giant oaks. I must admit that for a time I was lulled into an artificial serenity, partly because of the surroundings, but mostly because I was overdosed on sedatives and various forms of psychotic drugs.

But an unexpected side effect began to evidence itself. Somewhere deep within the recesses of my brain, memories of past infringements lay stored like aging bottles of wine.

For years alcohol and drugs had snaked through my cerebral arteries, building barriers between distasteful reality and a quixotic world all of my own. The pulling down of these barriers exposed truths that repulsed me. That caused me to confront the hopelessness of my lack of future. And worse, to confront a plethora of despicable deeds. If that was not enough, hours of cravings during the early stages of withdrawal contorted my body with agonizing spasms. It was more than I could bear.

I hated the clinic. I hated the confinement. I hated the cure.

And so I escaped through an open window and crawled back to the shadows and the security of oblivion found in alcohol and drugs. I wasn't yet thirty years old. A university graduate with a Masters in English and I had torpedoed a potentially bright future. I had not just fallen from grace but from the comforts of an upper-middle-class home. It seemed that all the education in the world was no defence against a disinterested mind and a disengaged attitude. I did, from time to time, experience an overwhelming sadness that my life had become worthless. But sadness is easily placated with a pill washed down in the company of a bottle of forty percent proof.

I had no friends, no close companions, and only nodding acquaintanceships with other nomads of the street. Like me, they were society's cast-offs, eking out an existence in states of paranoia and solipsism. There was a kind of comradeship, but only the type that develops amongst thieves; tolerance without trust. Many a night I had lapsed into a coma and woke in the morning to find my half-consumed bottle empty and any money scrounged off pedestrians that day, gone. Whenever I was sober enough to remember, I hid the cash in the lining of my jacket pocket.

And so my days were spent on corners begging. In the afternoons I roamed the lanes of the cities back streets stealing anything left unguarded.

One particular day had been a truly lean day.

Hunger gnawed my insides. I made my way to the city mission and joined the queue. The soup was watery and the meat served with a dollop of mash and a spoonful of peas, chewy. But it filled my stomach. It meant the meagre amount of coins rattling in my pocket could be used for gin.

The going down of the sun was the signal to make tracks to my spot in the park. Two bottles of the cheapest gin clinked in my knapsack. The shittiness of the day would be forgotten after half a bottle and I looked forward to that. On my way I stole a handful of chocolate bars from a dairy. Tonight would be like a party of sorts. My route led past the park fountain. It had once spewed a watery cascade over a mosaic of sunflowers but now sat in silent tribute to civic indifference. The greenish water now home to leaves, condoms, and mosquito larvae. My warm spot was thirty metres the other side.

But company awaited. I had seen the girl in the soup kitchen earlier. Her name was Alicia. That's all I knew. She sat on the tiled wall that circled the fountain. Eyes fixed on me.

"Whaddya think you're fucking looking at?"

She couldn't have been older than twenty but already looked fifty. An oversized yellow T-shirt under a black leather jacket hung down over grubby faded jeans.

"Go on. Get the fuck out of here."

Her voice rose several notches.

An elderly couple passing heard Alicia's rant. Their pace quickened. The man muttered to the worried face of his wife that he would call the police. This focused my mind. Mostly the cops left us down-and-outs alone as long as we left the good citizens alone. But this couple meant trouble. I needed to get Alicia out of sight.

I took a step to her side. Alicia eyed me up. Uncertainty creased her brow.

"What the fuck do you want, asshole?"

She rubbed her hands on her jeans. She kept rubbing. The glazed look told me she was high on something. But the agitation told me that she was now on the way down from whatever it had been. Maybe she was hallucinating and the same bugs that sometimes crawled over my body were now crawling over hers.

Her head slumped. This revealed a tattooed snake that wound its way up her back and curled around her neck. Dull eyes and two fangs signaled a warning not to come closer. Studs in her ears and nose and the gold ring looped through her lip bore testimony to a punk rocker marooned in a time when punk rock was long dead.

I had seen it all before. Alicia had fallen so far that even the brothels no longer had a place for her. My hand waved in the direction of the departing concerned citizens.

"The police are coming. You need to move away from here."

"I don't give a shit."

By the tremble in her voice and the shake of her head I knew she'd be craving a fix right now. Her mouth would be dry, head aching, and if she wasn't crashed into a torpid state quick smart, she'd soon be wailing like an Irish banshee until the police arrived.

I pulled the sack off my shoulder and showed her one of the gin bottles.

"I have two of these."

She reached for one.

"Give me the fucking thing."

"Not here. We need to go somewhere else."

A blank look into my face. Then a nod. She staggered to her feet, eyes now focused on the sot's Holy Grail dangling in front of her.

"Follow me," she said.

Her unsteady shuffle led me to the other side of the park and into a small graveyard. Picking a spot she sank to her knees. I dropped to the ground a few metres from her.

She looked across at me and forced a smile then tugged at the zipper of her jeans. I held up a hand.

"No. No sex."

An uncomprehending look. Then feral eyes darted side to side. Body tensed as if preparing for some unknown new threat.

"What the fuck do you want then?"

I passed the bottle. She snatched it. Eyes remained on me while she unscrewed the cap as if at any moment the precious liquid might be taken from her. She took a gulp and lowered the bottle to rest between her legs.

I relaxed and flicked the screw cap from the second bottle. With some relief I watched the tension fall away from her shoulders. Her head turned towards a lichen-covered upright slab of cracked marble.

"This is my friend Bartholomew Drefus," she said, pointing at it. "We've been friends for many years. Say hello. You can call him Barty if you like."

I read the name still visible beneath the spreading moss. Barty died in 1890.

"Barty listens to my troubles. He's like a father to me. Only he never comes into my room at night. Not Barty. Oh no, he's too much a of gentleman for that."

Alicia slumped sideways and leaned on her elbow. She managed the manoeuvre without upsetting the bottle.

We then lapsed into a silent vigil alongside Barty's grave and got drunk. Alcohol, the baptismal beverage for the uniting of fractured souls. With half-closed eyes I considered if it was possible that our two broken lives might make one half-decent human shell. By the time we both passed out neither of us could have given a shit.

###

As always I slept the sleep of the befuddled; comatose at the start and thereafter drifting in and out of consciousness, intermittently woken by my own snoring. The onset of dawn brought chirping and the beginnings of wakefulness. I had learnt never to sleep under a tree. Crapped on by a nervous squadron of feathered fighters was an experience I vowed not to repeat. However the tweeting was natures alarm clock only this clock could not be turned off. But I had grown used to morning sounds only this morning, something else. Singing. A woman's voice in a sweet lullaby.

Alicia was kneeling on the ground unloading what looked like possum skin hats from a plastic bag. I sat up to watch.

"Holy shit."

Alicia looked across at me and smiled. Two of her front teeth were missing.

"Are they kittens?" I asked.

She beamed like a child and nodded. The animals appeared to be quite dead. She lined five bodies in a row, then sat back on her haunches to admire her handiwork. For somebody inured to freakishness as I was, even this I found freaky. I needed to pee. I stood, half concealing myself behind a tree. Alicia didn't so much as glance my way. But my eyes remained on her.

"Why do you have dead kittens? Where did you find them?"

"This is what I do. I mend kittens. They're strays. Homeless. Just like you and me. No one wants them. No one feeds them. So I break their necks and bring them here."

For several seconds I stood statue-like, staring at the top of Alicia's bowed head. I zipped up my pants and turned back to her.

"Don't you... don't you mean you're *helping* them. You know? To a better place?"

Alicia's voice came at me in a scream. Spittle sprayed across her chin.

"No. *Mending*." A gurgling suck of breath. The glare that had just fired a thousand barbs softened. "*Helping* is taking old ladies across the street. This is not like that." She paused. "A nurse tends a patient. A vet fixes a dog. You know? When it can't have any more little dogs?" Her tone was now patient. She could have been a teacher explaining logic to an imbecile.

I nodded.

Alicia's gaze dropped once more to her furry charges.

"And when something is homeless like us, the spirit is broken. It's the same for the kittens. The homeless ones. The spirit is broken. And when something is broken, you mend it. That's the difference. You see that, don't you?"

In reality I wanted to scream that no, I did not see. But I nodded once more, fearful of another outburst if I didn't. Alicia produced a garden trowel and began to dig. I glanced around us. No one was watching. But then why would there be anyone else in the old cemetery? Nobody came here but junkies and mad people?

And Alicia was truly at home on both counts.

A bond developed between Alicia and me. I likened it to two wrecks looking for the same reef to crash on. For me it was a change from being alone. Our conversations were not particularly coherent. Years of addiction had curdled our brains. But somehow through hours of mumbled gibberish an understanding of a kind did grow between us. A symbiosis.

Each day I scrounged enough money to keep us in gin. But not drugs. For that, Alicia turned tricks. She used the water from the fountain to scrub herself up and from her second plastic bag produced a clean-ish top and skirt. She jumped guys in the back of cars for fifty bucks a time, sometimes for ten, Alicia never walked away empty-handed. Her earnings were never enough for anything stronger than weed. But it and the gin kept us on a tranquil plateau.

We were happy in a sad sort of way.

We ate every day at the city mission.

On a morning no different from any other at the mission, someone stole Alicia's bag. She totally flipped and ran through the streets screaming for its return. When her limited energy levels finally failed her she slumped onto the pavement and howled like a wolf under a full moon. Her bag held all her worldly possessions. And, worse, without the top and skirt she wouldn't be able to present her pitiful body to earn a dollar.

We made our way back to Barty. Alicia wrapped her arms around Barty's gravestone and sobbed. I had two bottles of gin hidden in the bushes. I gave her one then sat back against a headstone a few metres away and slurred a greeting to Mrs Beatrice Donald and her two daughters.

Alicia explained her predicament to Barty. It was like watching a small child. Fragile. Innocent. After a time she stopped crying. She had gulped down half a bottle of gin and drifted into a coma. I was grateful that Barty could comfort her. With a sense of surprise I discovered her distress was distressing me. I had long ago begun to believe I could no longer feel emotion when faced with human tragedy.

I made a decision. I would find the money to replace Alicia's belongings. Recapping my bottle I lay it on the ground beside her then walked off towards the city.

Thankfully, despite the warnings, some people still had faith in today's society.

I stole the first bicycle I came across.

Three kilometres of cycling almost exhausted me, but I did make it to my destination.The iron-gate swung open with only the faintest squeak of protest. I stood under the drooping willow branches lining the drive and peered through the foliage at the two-storey house. My childhood home. Evening was approaching and lights were on, but the drapes had not been drawn. No movement anywhere that I could detect. That didn't surprise me. My mother would be in the kitchen baking and my father would be in the lounge watching the news on TV.

A rough brush down of my jeans and a buff of the toes of my shoes against my denim legs would do. I had used the water tap in the public ablutions block on the beach to wash grime from my face and hands. An attempt to comb the knots from my hair, failed. The beard remained a tangle.

In this house there would be no welcoming arms for a wayward son. Few memories of my childhood came to mind and those that did were not joyous. No warm fuzzy feelings – the early years had seen to that.

But the thought didn't faze me. I needed money for Alicia. When I had it I'd be gone.

I walked up to the back door and knocked softly. It opened.

My mother's reaction was as expected. Stunned. Uncomprehending.

"Hey, Mum."

I smiled and feigned a positive front that did battle with my true feelings. My mother saw through it, beard and all. Her face settled into a display of worry lines. She rubbed her hands on her apron.

"What are you doing here Jimmy?" She glanced behind her - an instinctive reaction. She feared my father, as I had done all through my childhood. Her voice dropped to a whisper. "You shouldn't have come."

Turning, she walked back into the kitchen. She didn't slam the door so I took that as some kind of invitation to follow. Her back was still to me as she fiddled with a knob on the stove. She stooped and opened and closed the oven door. The delaying tactics were not working. I wasn't going anywhere and she knew it. Not yet anyway.

Finally she gave up the pretense and confronted me. Leaning forward and grasping the sides of the wooden mobile bench. Her knuckles whitened, matching the blotchy spattering of flour across her face. For as long as I could remember, my mother's face was covered in flour and the kitchen smelled of freshly baked cookies, just as it did now.

Shortbread was my guess. A tray covered with a tea-towel sat on the bench top.

"I need some money. I had nowhere else to go."

Mother bowed her head. The inner demons were at work. Fighting the urge to turn her son away and fighting the desire to hold him to her breast. I knew this inner conflict because I had witnessed it many times. I should have felt shame but I felt nothing. All of that had been lost a long time ago somewhere in the city gutters with my vomit and my urine.

A mighty bang of a door behind us.

My father entered the kitchen. The slamming of the door had doubtless been an attempt to intimidate me. When I was younger, he used to beat me with his fists. Once he'd broken a rod over my back. Life before I grew strong was unbearable. But I did grow strong. Lifting weights after school built muscle. The gang kids taught me to box. When the time came, I beat the shit out of my father. It was a lesson never forgotten. Father never raised his hand to me again. That was a few weeks before I left home.

Of course, now I was a drunken junkie with a permanent crazy look. I could see the fear in his eyes. I looked at the block of wood on the bench that held the knives. He followed my gaze and shrank away. He looked as if he wanted to run.

I suppressed a smile. I needed money and gloating would not open his wallet. Father's widened eyes came back to my face.

"What are you doing here? Don't tell me. Money. It's always money."

I nodded.

"Look at you."

I stepped forward.

He stepped back.

"You going to hit me, you little shit. Go on, try it. "

"Bernie, leave him," Mum said. "He's your son. No matter what."

"He's not my son. My son was a fine, wonderful young man. He was athletic, intelligent, had a great future. My son was not a doped-out drunken bum stealing from his family, his friends and anyone else who tried to help him. My son was not a gutless loser. My son was not a disgusting piece of stinking garbage. That son died and it broke my heart. God will punish you! Do you hear me! Repent, Godammit!"

And there it was, the doctrine that had hounded me throughout my childhood. I had broken his heart. What a crock of shit. How many times had I been dragged before the pastor of our church? How many times had I been humiliated in front of the congregation? How many times did he tell me he loved me as he beat me until my screams became soundless, gagging? And my mother, my darling mother watched, sobbing, but holding still. She never interfered.

Well, fuck them both.

My father did what he always did. Pulled out his wallet and threw money on the floor. I bent down and scooped it up then turned and walked out. Neither of them tried to stop me and I never said thank you.

###

As I cycled back to the cemetery I drifted into a pensive mood. Thoughts rattled round in my head to the rhythm of the squeaking back wheel. The level of sobriety throughout the last few hours was testing my psyche. I had pedaled through purgatory to confront my parents and now, as always, the fortitude of then was surrendering to weakness. As I cycled through the shopping center, giant shadowy tentacles lashed out at me like a ploughman's whip, slapping at me and finally entangling me in a net of sociopathic disorder. An insistent chorus of a thousand voices propelled me through the door of a bottle store. By the time I made it back to the cemetery I had blown Alicia's money on gin and cocaine.

Utopia was now only a snort away.

Alicia had her arms wrapped around Barty's headstone. A needle lay on the ground beside her. She had mainlined her emergency stash.

I let the bike fall to the ground and sat with my back against Ethel Blacksmith's headstone. She had died in 1896. I screwed the top off the gin bottle and gulped down two mouthfuls, then trickled some coke along the back of my hand and sniffed.

"Who the fuck are *you*?" Alicia slurred, only one eye managing to open. "What are you doing with my bike?" A finger pointed at me. Then her arm dropped to her side. "Go somewhere else. This is my home."

There was no surprise that she'd forgotten I was trying to help her. Junkies have no recall. No humanity even. Alicia's head fell to her chest. Eyes glazed. Her body contorted knocking the gin bottle over. The contents spewed onto the ground.

"Nooooo," she cried.

It was too late. She held it up by the neck and dribbled the last dregs into her mouth.

The empty bottle was tossed at me. I lacked the wit to dodge.

"Hey." I rubbed my upper thigh. "What are you doing?"

"I have nothing," she cried out and began to weep. She curled into the fetal position and sucked on her thumb like a baby. A light breeze caught a few leaves and blew them across her body. And at that exact moment a flush of moonlight splashed across her face. Nature was comforting this poor soul.

In that moment I knew what was happening. Alicia was being soothed by the hand of God. I hadn't seen it before, but the coke made it all so clear. God had sent me a message. He was showing me what needed to be done. He was reaching out for this forlorn child of heaven. He was expecting me to guide her to His very own realm of peace and tranquility.

Kneeling beside Alicia I pulled her across my lap. She offered no resistance. I closed my hands around her neck.

And squeezed.

She thrashed about and the eyes of her tattooed snake bulged, but in the end its fangs were as ineffective as Alicia's life had been.

I stayed watching until her grave was filled. When the men had gone, I moved forward and placed a flower on the mound.

Everyone deserved a flower.

It felt good having helped Alicia. She was now free from pain. Free from suffering. And in the company of her friend Barty. What an exhilarating and rewarding experience it had been to perform such an act of care.

Droplets of rain fell upon my face. A cleansing. Clarity of thought surged though me. The imperative was clear. To help other people who knew suffering like Alicia into the Kingdom of Heaven. Alicia would understand. It would be like mending kittens.

I rose to my feet and looked at the stars.

"I hear you God," I shouted. "I hear you."

When my euphoria had waned and I could think it all through, it occurred to me there were no two souls more tortured than my parents.

My eyes fell to the bike.

The End

CPSIA information can be obtained at www.ICGtesting.com
Printed in the USA
LVOW10s1602100515

437947LV00001B/21/P